Horses In the Yard (and Other Equestrian Dilemmas)

Horses In the Yard (and Other Equestrian Dilemmas)

Joanne M. Friedman

iUniverse, Inc.
New York Lincoln Shanghai

Horses In the Yard (and Other Equestrian Dilemmas)

Copyright © 2007 by Joanne M. Friedman

All rights reserved. No part of this book may be used or reproduced by any means, graphic, electronic, or mechanical, including photocopying, recording, taping or by any information storage retrieval system without the written permission of the publisher except in the case of brief quotations embodied in critical articles and reviews.

iUniverse books may be ordered through booksellers or by contacting:

iUniverse
2021 Pine Lake Road, Suite 100
Lincoln, NE 68512
www.iuniverse.com
1-800-Authors (1-800-288-4677)

Because of the dynamic nature of the Internet, any Web addresses or links contained in this book may have changed since publication and may no longer be valid.

The views expressed in this work are solely those of the author and do not necessarily reflect the views of the publisher, and the publisher hereby disclaims any responsibility for them.

ISBN: 978-0-595-46285-8 (pbk)
ISBN: 978-0-595-90582-9 (ebk)

Printed in the United States of America

Contents

Introduction: Horses in the Yard vii
Chapter 1:   You Are Here → X 1
Chapter 2:   It's All Your Fault! 4
Chapter 3:   Horse Therapists 9
Chapter 4:   Women Overcoming: Force vs. Finesse 14
Chapter 5:   Starting Over 18
Chapter 6:   Come Into the Light 23
Chapter 7:   Left in the Lust 28
Chapter 8:   Buyers and Sellers 33
Chapter 9:   Dumb Human Tricks 101 38
Chapter 10: The Five Horses We Meet on Earth 42
Chapter 11: Little Big Horse 50
Chapter 12: My Horse Hates Me! 60
Chapter 13: AndThenThereWas … Synchronicity! 66
Chapter 14: Psych! 70
Chapter 15: That's "Latent", Not "Lazy" Learning 75
Chapter 16: In Defense of the Pros 81
Chapter 17: Real Horse TV! 84
Chapter 18: The Breeding Bug 87
Chapter 19: Stuff and Nonsense 95

Chapter 20: Talk to the Hoof 98
Chapter 21: The Vet's Point-of-View 108
Chapter 22: Strange Equine Afflictions 113
Chapter 23: This Old Horse 121
Chapter 24: Messy Endings 128
Chapter 25: Epilogue 132

Introduction: Horses in the Yard

There are a lot of books available on the subject of horse training, horse health, horse bonding, horse husbandry, rider training, and riding equipment. Everything Horse seems to have been covered. Who needs another horse book?

If you ride horses, this book is for you. If you're thinking about buying a horse, this book is for you. If you've bought a horse and are wondering why, this book is for you. If you have a few questions you're afraid to ask, this book is for you. If you want a good laugh at the expense of all of the people just listed, this book is definitely for you.

Most of all, this book is for the kind-hearted folks who have succumbed to their childhood dream of horses grazing in the back yard. You, of all horse people, need a shoulder to cry on and a good dose of fellowship. Horses are great companions, but living with them can be a lonely way to go.

When you're staring out your kitchen window at the paddock where you put the horses, and the horses are nowhere to be seen, and there's no one you can call to share the frustration, the desire to pack it all in can be overwhelming. Stronger people than you have simply thrown a suitcase in the car and a bale of hay on the lawn and headed for parts unknown.

The first time you try to get Loverboy to load on the trailer, you may be overjoyed that he's so willing. When he politely declines a repeat performance for the trip home, you may wonder if you're going to have to live at the show grounds forever. Removing the lead rope and singing "Born Free" as the errant gelding trots off into the sunset isn't the answer, but it's a strong temptation.

Even if the horses in question are in someone else's yard for safe keeping, there will be times when you will stand aghast, staring at the creatures you thought you knew, and wondering what you did to deserve whatever they're doing in retribution.

My horseshoer once spoke the truest words I've ever heard: "It doesn't make sense to piss off a thousand pound animal who's going to remember you the next time you meet." There are better ways to accomplish what you've set out to do. If you can't find one, then maybe you're headed in the wrong direction.

You won't find salvation among these pages, but if the advice, stories and cautionary tales can help you regain your sense of humor, offer suggestions for change, and allow you to balance the bad against the much greater good, then I've done what I set out to do, and that's all I can hope for.

As for who I am to give advice and point out the follies of this horse life, I am a horseperson with forty-odd (very) years' experience. I own and operate Gallant Hope Farm in northwest New Jersey, write a column for an online horse magazine for which I've also done web seminars on basic horsemanship, tack, and my real forte, clicker training, and have contributed articles to *America's Horse* and horse stories to several anthologies. The horse humor guest column that formed the basis for my first book, *It's a Horse's Life (Advice and Observations For the Humans Who Choose to Share It,* iUniverse, 2003) ran in the *Boston Herald* local papers. I have degrees in psychology and education. I've trained, cared for, ridden, shown English and Western and been injured by the best. I have more horses than common sense, and love every minute of this horse life.

Read on and know that you are not alone.

Wanna play? Just do me a favor and open the gate, would you?

Chapter 1

You Are Here → X

Every once in a while, each of us, who has bit the bullet and bought a farm, is asked—usually by non-horsy types—why we do what we do. They stand there in their clean clothes, spotlessly coiffed, and stare into our eyes, hoping to put a name to the form of our insanity. What would cause an otherwise intelligent person to give up all hope of a normal schedule? What is there in us that sends us scrabbling for grubby jeans in the pre-dawn gloom, while our fellows are sipping lattes, waiting for the Sun God to flip open their smooth eyelids? Can we justify forgetting where we left our youngest child in our haste to get home to stand with Leos Loophole while the farrier trims his sensitive feet? Why *do* we do this?

In forty years, the frequency of that question rivals the number of times I've said, "Zipper, if you grab my sleeve *one more time ...!*" I've asked it of myself on cold winter days when pneumonia wasn't sufficient excuse to let the horses go without grain. On low-energy days, I've asked it of my farm-owning friends. The answers—mine and theirs—are usually vague and couched in shrugs and chuckles.

"I had too much money and really wanted to see what poverty felt like."

"The smell keeps my relatives from coming to stay."

"No one has asked me to chaperone a field trip since I bought the place."

"I can leave boring parties early without anyone complaining, because everyone thinks I have to get up at dawn."

I'm not going to be the one to criticize anyone else's reasons. This horse thing is very personal. Like politics and religion, it's something that requires a certain suspension of disbelief and does not bear up under close scrutiny. Still, leaving questions unanswered somehow cuts across the grain, so I feel pressed to find a suitable, universally comprehensible, explanation for this impossibly complex decision.

It's been a long and utterly demoralizing winter. With no indoor facilities at my disposal, I am forced, under such circumstances, to put mounted activities on hold and focus on survival for the duration. Each year I spend the bulk of the cold months trying to make the job easier. It's a creative endeavor that gives me great comfort.

Thankfully, even the longest winter has to end. With spring at hand, even the mud shows signs of giving up to my passionate desire to ride. The horses are eager to be rid of winter jackets and the hair that is coming out in merry handfuls like dark confetti at a May Day party. They kick up their heels and race around the pasture, unchained at last.

I share their joy. Day by day and one by one I shed the puffy, waterproof layers of yard goods that have protected me through the icy morning feedings. I pull out the dresser drawer where my light, cool summer schooling breeches are stuffed and dump them out on the floor. The ones unworthy of reclamation hit the trash immediately. The rest are neatly folded. My favorites slide past my post-winter thighs without complaint or criticism, and off I go with a step ten pounds lighter.

And with that, I know the answer! I pull on my jacket as my feet slide into my rubber clogs, and recognize an air of excitement. It's not, I realize, about the spring, but about survival. Together, my horses and I have made it through another threatening winter. We have taken life, not in the huge chunks favored by the folks who know what a PDA is and how to use it, but in tiny, moment-by-moment increments. The minute or so it took to hike through the ice and sleet to the trough and verify the demise of the de-icer was monumental to my furry friends and me. The daily ritual trip up and down the barn aisle, assessing moods and conditions, cooing softly and hearing their nickering response was hugely potent. Experimental blanket repairs with new materials, sending for prices on radiant heaters for the wash stall to forestall next years' mid-winter injury issues, collecting piles of brochures on new feeds and the latest wormers, these are the winter rituals that connect my too-civilized world to the wild one across the fence. My friends are depending on me, and the challenge is what gets me out of bed in the morning.

My friends! How fortunate are we to be able to look out our windows and see our best friends looking back? Never mind that I'm still sporting an unaccounted-for bruise on my upper arm. Whichever horse did that, it was not with malice aforethought, of that I can be sure. My little herd is kind of heart, stalwart of spirit, and here for the duration.

So to those who ask why, I say, "Because it keeps me alive!" To those who say, "Well, that's pretty lame" I say, "Yeah? So?" and off I go, my favorite breeches forgiving my winter lapse and my best friends waiting to party with me, dancing to the tune of grain *shushing* into buckets and worshipping me for the magic of the tack room cookie bin as intensely as I worship them for their intimate and elemental connection to the world. I can't help but wonder what the PDA folks do at 6 AM that rivals this.

Chapter 2

▼

It's All Your Fault!

If you've been following the trend towards the "natural" in horsemanship, you have probably come to the conclusion—and rightly so—that whatever problems your horse has, whether under saddle, from the ground, or in the herd, have been caused by your ignorance. It's all true. Unless you've got a degree from the Horse Institute conferred on you by the members of your herd for Obvious Horse-ness Above and Beyond Your Humanity, you are doing pretty much everything wrong.

Just recently an article in a glossy horse magazine reinforced for all of us round-penner-wannabees that gentle chewing during a training session means that the horse has settled in and is learning what you wanted him to learn. A sign of relaxation, the author said, and something to strive for. No sooner had that issue hit the stands than someone in the crowd jumped in to negate that theory and screw us all up. The author of the letter to the editor contended that horses do that chewing thing when they are frightened or stressed, *not* when they are happy and learning. Oh, *no!* Discord among the naturalists is the last thing we simple-minded novices need. We just got used to the idea that horses want us to be part of their herd and spend quality time grazing with them in the pasture (the laughter you hear isn't really your horse; it's your neighbors behind the shrubbery). We just quit our jobs and organized our lives around baking healthy horse cookies and practicing equine body language. Now we are being told that we are doing it all wrong … again!

Not one for trusting human opinion when I can get the down-and-dirty straight from the horses' mouths, I took this notion to my advisory committee in the lower pasture. The new mini, Hair I Come, came rushing up offering opinions on anything I'd care to ask. He poked his nose in my crotch, mugged my pocket, noticed the lack of cookies and hustled back to his post under the Appy gelding. "But what about the chewing issue?"

"Chewing?" he sniffed. "You want chewing; bring cookies."

Zips Idiocy looked me square in the eye as he always does and waited. I pointed at his shoulder; he stretched his leg on cue. I checked for chewing. There was a little. I stuck my hand in his mouth and retrieved my hat. The chewing stopped.

The rest of the herd wanted no part of my poll, so I had to wait for an opportune moment to put the theory to the test under cover of training. As soon as the ice melted enough to warrant actually getting on a horse, I saddled up Zip and took him for a mid-winter's walk in the ring. Before the ice-up, we'd been working on simple stuff like "on the bit", "walking in a straight line" and "get off my foot". Figuring the best bet for quick chewing response was to go back to his last successful venture, I stood him by the mounting block. I went after him and stood him by the mounting block again, clicking my clicker and handing out carrots. I got off the mounting block and moved his rear end back where it belonged, where I could actually reach his back from the mounting block. I got off the mounting block, backed him up, took the cone out of his mouth, and parked him in place again. All the while, I watched for chewing.

At last, just as I ran out of carrots, he stood quietly, dropped his head and chewed gently. Score!

I'm no expert, as is quite apparent, but it seemed to me that his chewing was directly related to the fact that he'd had his joke, and he was ready for riding. This happened in the barn aisle, too. I'd finally gotten the last of the bridle straps out of his mouth (he's got the quickest teeth in the East), reached a level of frustration known only to mothers of potty-resistant three-year-old humans, and was just about to blow when he dropped his head and did the chewing thing.

Now, that's not to say that *all* horses chew when they've finally pushed their owners as close to the edge as they dare without risking retribution, but in Zip's case, that's the story. In fact, having spent Zip's entire life with him, I am willing to bet my new Ariats that it's a direct off-shoot of the infantile mouthing sign that I saw him use so often to indicate to whichever herd member he'd irritated into attacking him that he was only kidding. "I'm just a baby! You can't beat me up; that's foal abuse!"

Not wanting to be called on the fact that I only had one subject in my experiment, rendering the sample limited if not useless, I tried each of the others in turn. The Mini Mite chews when he thinks treats are coming. He can be standing peacefully mugging the new Appy and hear the rustle of the carrot bag, and instantly, even as he's hustling his fuzzy body to the location of the food, the chewing begins.

Leo Linkletter, herd MC, chews in preparation for an assault on Mini Marvin's fleece wither protector.

Pokey Loves Me chews all the time. She's in chronic adoration mode, and chews if she even thinks one of her people might be somewhere nearby. Or one of her horse friends. Or a chunk of blanket that resembles the profile of her favorite stud.

Pinky the One-Eyed Wonder App and his similarly Appy buddy, Sunny, never chew. Ever. Unless there's actual food in their mouths, they simply don't waste the energy. They will stick their noses into whatever intrigues them and follow directions with great enthusiasm, but random, unnecessary chewing just isn't in their stash of responses.

So, having enlarged my sample to six, I think it's safe to say that it's never safe to say anything definitive about horses, and that, however roundabout it may appear, is exactly the point I was getting at. Unless I've somehow lucked into a life's worth of the most forgiving horses on the planet, it just doesn't matter if we don't do everything right. They seem, for whatever demented reason, to like us. They like being with us. They let us ride them, for heaven's sake!

Do we screw up? Monumentally! Like the time I tried to force my Quarter Horse mare into a trailer for the first time using a rope around her butt and the business end of a broom. I had *Novice* stamped on my forehead, all right. After several hours of poking and prodding, cajoling and bribing, she simply walked away. So did I.

But two days later, after one of my fellow boarders had taken pity on me and given me a video about trailer loading, I brazenly walked right up to that mare, did a little of what I thought I understood from the tape, and bingo! We never had a trailer loading problem again, despite my stupidity. We had a few other problems, but not that one.

The key, I believe, is to relax and try to see things through your horse's eyes. If that's not possible—and many of us are truly vision-impaired in that regard—just take it slow and set small goals. You don't need to have a horse that lies down on command. You can get by with one that doesn't bite you every time you pass within reach. Baby steps. It may be all your fault, but if you can keep the errors small enough, even the horse might not care.

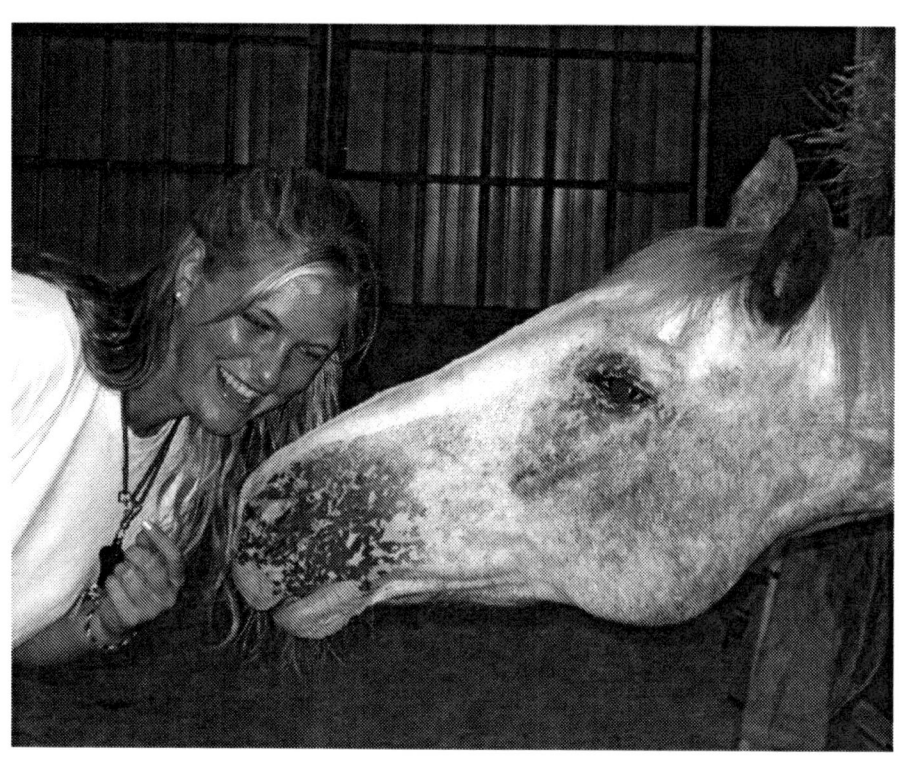

Bad day? The Horse Doctor is In.

Chapter 3

Horse Therapists

There is a movement afoot among humans desperate for a cure to their many and varied ills to turn to the natural world around them for help. A few years ago, no one was talking about bringing dogs (or cats, or ferrets, or baby elephants) into hospitals. Nursing home residents had to be satisfied with the occasional teen church group or elementary school class to visit, or they were stuck watching *The People's Court* until their breathing ceased along with their intelligence. Patients in for long-term hospitalization had nothing to look forward to but their occasional sponge baths. Depression and anxiety ran rampant in institutions everywhere.

Then one day someone somewhere was stroking their resident pet-of-choice, and in mid-reverie was stuck by the thought that what felt good to them might also feel good to people in places where such contact was more difficult to come by. Bingo! A movement was born.

I had hoped to find a reference that would name names and put a date on the blessed event, but, like so many miracles, this one seems to have popped onto the scene without benefit of any chicken-and-egg debate. Regardless of the genesis, hearty congratulations are due to the first hospital administrator to say "yes" to having a puppy visit the pediatrics ward. Someone should be thanked for letting kittens live in nursing homes. And whoever came up with the little rubber shoes that allow ponies and miniature horses to wander the halls of the most desolate of homes-away-from-home should be raised on a pedestal and treated to dinner and a movie at the very least.

What every *real* animal lover knows is that we only pretend that our relationships with our pets are for their benefit. In reality, there's nothing more helpful than a companion animal when it comes to untangling the knotted fishing line that is the typical human life. If you've been in the company of a cat, then you know that they have an amazing ability to switch gears without all the *sturm und drang* that accompanies such changes in the human mind. A cat can be sound asleep, and while you're still marveling at his ability to sleep upside down on top of the TV, he can make an electrifying leap across the room, smack the dog on the ear, shred the sofa, and disappear. If you follow the path of destruction, you will find him asleep again, curled up in your purse, or stretched full-length along the headboard of the bed. Or you simply may not see him for a day or two. There's no aftermath, no grudges held, no explanations and no concern for appearances.

What horse lovers know is that we humans can never hope to be as kind, open and connected as our horses most definitely are. Our biggest problem is that we are so incredibly busy and ego-centric that we rarely stop ranting and raving long enough to notice that someone else is talking. That someone may well be the horse in the stall in the barn at the end of the driveway.

Since we don't listen, horses and other animals have learned ways to get our attention. Fussbudget Leo, for instance, has been trying to get across to me for ages that he does not consider me the sharpest tack in the box. He has lived with me for some eight years now, and I've only recently realized that he is fairly convinced that, left to my own devices, I'll get both of us eaten by something large, sharp-fanged and probably airborne. I don't, he says, know anything about safe weather; ice, being, in his opinion, my particular blind spot. So, after several days of snow, rain and below-freezing temperatures, Leo asked to be allowed to stay in the barnyard, safe on relatively dry ground, for the rest of the day. I'm not stubborn, so I allowed him his way that day. The next day, I carefully tested the footing before turning the herd loose to make their way to the pasture. Leo paused at the barn door, sniffed the ground, glared at me over his shoulder with a "Surely you jest!" expression, and tried to turn back. I reminded him that he is, after all, a horse, and I'd already checked for ice. "You'll be fine," I assured him. "Hmpfh!" he said. He left, obviously disgruntled. His nose close to the suspect ground, he slowly picked his way across the barnyard, made one last stab at sympathy at the gate, then sighed and wandered out.

This morning, after I once again visibly checked for ice and jumped up and down to demonstrate the high safety rating of the footing outside the door, Leo made an even stronger argument for the indoor life. In the back of the barn is a large pile of loose sawdust bedding. It nearly reaches the height of the floor of the loft—nine and a half feet at last measurement—and fills a 10 x 20 foot space. With a sly glance in my direction, Leo scaled Mount Sawdust. His front feet wound up about 6 feet up before he ran out of headroom, while his butt end lingered closer to the ground. There he stood, very still, not looking at me, hoping I wouldn't notice a big, chestnut chunk of sawdust in the pile. Could he have spoken any more loudly?

As I stood laughing, the thought crossed my mind that Leo would make a great therapy horse, not because he is such an adept communicator, but because he is so obviously in need of therapy. If any horse would empathize with the ill, infirm and insane, it would be Leo.

This thought was still percolating when I attended a party where much younger drunk people did odd things with canapés. Between the jell-o shots and the chili dip, I was approached by a relatively normal young woman—a friend of my daughter's—who wanted my help in the form of business cards. I'm known far and wide for my willingness to produce cheap (read "free") business cards on my computer, so this was not an unusual request.

As we talked, however, it came to (dim) light that this lovely young lady was a guardian angel at a group home for severely developmentally disadvantaged (what used to be called "retarded") adults. The light bulb glowed brighter as the jell-o shots wore off. What about, I suggested, a field trip to my farm for her charges? She was all for it, and a deal was struck for the following week.

To say I was nervous would be akin to saying the White House is government-issue housing. My plan was to have the horses in their stalls, with Zip locked behind a strong door to prevent his trying to drag one of the unfortunate visitors in for a quick hug and kiss. Where it would go from there was anyone's guess. I suspected that the most likely candidate for unflappable huggery would be the old Standardbred, Grady, so his stall was first on my agenda. Beyond that, I was keeping my fingers crossed that a divine hand (or soft nose) would guide me.

The visitors arrived with much fanfare. Jen—self-designated "wrangler"—hauled her charges out of the customized van and onto the driveway. Only two of the residents of the group home had been available for the visit, which was exactly the right number as there were two wranglers and one very worried farm owner to attend to them and to the nine horses, whose curiosity was already beginning to show in nickers and whinnies.

One of the visitors was almost entirely blind and deaf; the other less disabled, but still difficult to move into the barn. Obviously I hadn't planned this well enough, or I would have asked whether the ramp to the aisle would present a problem. Jen, however, was undaunted. Chattering a mile a minute, she wrestled her people into the barn, and there we stood. The group eyed the horses, and the horses eyed right back.

At this point I have to interject that anyone who doubts the intuitive intellect of horses should try this experiment for themselves. My horses are good; of that there is no doubt. They are by no means perfect. In fact, when I told my daughter (after the fact, of course) that her gelding, Grady, had been my first choice for an up-close nose patting session, she was shocked. I, however, have great faith in my horses' ability to sense what is needed and step up to the plate … as long as there are no squirrels or horse-eating garbage cans nearby.

The female visitor, deaf and blind, panicked immediately. For the next twenty minutes she clung to her wrangler and shrieked. This was not a little shriek. This was a horse-deafening keening sound that made *me* want to run into my stall and hide. The male, on the other hand, was a laugher.

He chuckled and merrily slapped Grady repeatedly between the eyes. My heart was in my brain, so I was unable to sort out the best course for the prevention of bodily harm to anyone present.

The horses were not so indisposed. It took me a minute to realize that Grady was standing perfectly still, being walloped between the eyes with abandon, and loving it. The shrieker was going at it loud and long, but the horses weren't batting an eye. Even Dolly Don't Touch Me watched with curiosity from the dark recesses of her stall.

When I could breathe again, I stood fascinated as the horses, heads hanging over their stall guards, nudged and jostled the visitors ever so gently for their attention. One by one I brought them out, following Grady with the chronically maternal Paint mare and the Arabian pony. I hadn't actually forgotten Leo, but I wasn't actively mentally competent enough to really remember the original plan.

As I stood holding the Paint mare's head, I felt a soft snurffle on my cheek. Leo had stretched his neck to its limit over his stall guard and was giving me little horsy kisses. I turned to look at him and saw the biggest, softest eyes I've ever seen on a horse. These were not Leo's usual eyes. He's an aging Quarter Horse, and he has one of the most expressive faces I've ever seen, but a soft eye like the one I saw that day has not been among his favorite looks. These eyes were so full of understanding and pleading, I was startled. Of course I invited him out for a turn, and he was delighted to be slapped between the eyes by a gleeful visitor to the rhythm of the incessant shrieking from the end of the barn.

Why? Who knows? For my part, I want to believe that Leo and the other horses actually sensed some kinship with their disabled visitors. Perhaps Jen's charges were closer to the horses than I'll ever be. Maybe there's a level of intuition that crosses boundaries and that we can never hope to really understand. Whatever the explanation, the experience was electric, and it will go down in memory as one of the most exciting horse moments of my life. All this is by way of saying that we mustn't underestimate our equines. What they have to offer is more than we can possibly imagine. We need, from time to time, to step back and allow them the courtesy of showing us what they can do. After all, who died and left us boss?

Chapter 4

▼

Women Overcoming: Force vs. Finesse

No book about horses and sanity would be complete without a chapter on how working with horses can help women overcome such negative tendencies as shyness, subservience, and poor self-image. Perhaps reeking of horse isn't the best route to popularity in some social circles, but the experience of cooperative work with an animal as big and sometimes scary as a horse can really give a woman a leg up on her internal quandaries.

Elsewhere in this book I have described the intense experience of watching my horses accurately read and react to severely developmentally disadvantaged adults whose communication skills would be considered by most to be non-existent. It was that moment when my horses queued up for a chance to be whacked and shrieked at by strangers that drove home something I'd learned and long since forgotten. Animals are close to nature. In fact, one might argue that they *are* nature. Likewise, humans stripped of the false trappings of social standing and self-importance reach a natural level the rest of us might give our Gucci bags to achieve if we were aware that such a thing existed.

One thing the majority of women have in common is that we are physically smaller than most men. Before you rush to your computer to refute that, note the careful use of "most" and "the majority". Sorry, but this is the way the world is. Women are built differently from men, and I'm not talking obvious body parts. A man's center of gravity is in his upper torso. That's why Christopher Reeve toppled so disastrously from his horse and was lawn-darted into a rock wall. A man's weight is in his chest.

A woman's on the other hand, is in her (sorry) hindquarters. This is a good thing for riding's sake as it allows a woman to ground significantly more thoroughly in the saddle than a man can. She's less likely to lose her balance and topple nose-first (though a slow slide down the neck of her favorite steed is not out of the question) unless she's picked up bad "perching" habits that we'll get to later. A woman who can imagine being a half-empty (or half-full, depending on her level of optimism) sack of grain can sit in a saddle with a security and balance few men can achieve. This is one of several reasons for the predominance of women in all phases of the horse world.

Looking at the physical conformation issue more closely, it's also obvious that a man's muscle mass is centered in his chest, upper arms and thighs. A woman's muscle mass is centered elsewhere, in the same place as her center of gravity but far less welcome there. This center-body strength is necessary for child-bearing. A man would find it difficult at best to get through a day with a twenty-pound weight strapped to his belly. His back and buttock muscles would be hard-pressed to support it. When pregnant husbands are given the fake belly to wear to simulate their wives' situation in hopes of fostering a little compassion, the contraption is hung from shoulder straps, not belted on. I haven't done the research, but I'd be willing to bet that women weight-lifters are better at the clean-and-jerk than at the overhead press. It's not a matter of sexism but one of sex.

So, all that considered, it's also apparent that a woman will have good balance on the ground but probably be lacking the upper-body strength that would allow her to overpower either a man or a horse. That's where finesse kicks in. What women can't do with force, they learn to do through finesse. I know better than to try to throw a forty-pound hay bale using my shoulders and upper arms. I've spent enough time on the ground under such misguided loads to realize that I'm better off using my legs and lower body strength to bull the weight into position. No matter how much time I spend at the gym, I will never be able to significantly alter the balance of muscle in my body. And that's okay. It's when women try to fight nature that terrible situations arise.

Enter Horse as Purveyor of Emotional Strength.

The average horse weighs in at around 1000 pounds. That's a big animal. It's certainly bigger than the average human, male or female. That's 1000 pounds of prey animal facing 140 pounds of predator, and wondering whether he'll survive the interaction. What makes a face-to-face with a horse so empowering, however, isn't that we are able, with a few harsh words or a swipe with a whip, to force him to comply with our demands. What's so empowering is that he will comply because he's *not* afraid. He will comply when he realizes there is no threat implied or intended by our presence. He responds because he is in need of a leader, and he has elected us to the post.

It's not automatic, this election process. He has to decide based on our behavior that we are smart enough, sane enough, and alert enough to keep this new herd of two out of harm's way. It's up to us to show him we're capable.

The woman recovering from abuse or other stressful life situations may feel she's in no way in charge of anything, least of all her own world. She faces the horse with trepidation. The horse senses the fear and becomes tense and concerned. The wise instructor (teaching frightened adults was my stock-in-trade for a while, so I count myself in that group) starts small. The woman is handed a soft brush and sent to fuss over the horse. It's pointed out that if she stands close to the animal, she will be out of range of a well-aimed kick. She is warned to watch for tell-tale signs of fear in herself and the horse. She's warned to keep her feet out from under the horse's stomping hoof. They're both allowed to back away and regroup and try again until they reach an accord regarding personal space. Calm prevails, and within a few minutes, hours or sessions, interaction becomes friendship. It happens almost every time a woman is allowed enough time and space to work through the situation.

So a woman whose daily life is overwhelming her learns to step back. Is this a cure for her endless problems? Of course not. Simple is not simplistic.

One woman arrived at the farm with an intense desire to learn to ride and more emotional and physical problems than most could bear. Her first lesson ended with her sitting in the saddle while the horse walked in a circle in a small pen. She shook so hard her teeth clattered. The horse understood and never made a wrong step. For a year this continued. Health problems caused her to miss sessions, but she always came back. In time she stopped shaking. Her boyfriend bought her "real" riding clothes, and she began talking about becoming a jumper. What a transformation!

She never did jump. Her sessions ended when our trainer moved out of state, but the sense of empowerment, the calmness that she exuded, were a fine outcome.

Finesse. We don't need power or the ability to instill fear in order to survive. We can learn from our horses that mindful existence is all that's necessary, and it's available to anyone willing to give up force to gain empowerment.

Chapter 5

▼

Starting Over

Spring is just around the corner. Punxatawny Phil has been unceremoniously dragged from his groundhog hutch by a top-hatted Town Father, and he's shown us his shadow. Six more weeks of winter await, then spring will be upon us.

This having been an unusually long and gloriously erratic winter, it's been difficult to ignore the opening strains of spring's song. When the temperature soared into double digits (that's Fahrenheit, by the way), I fought the urge to strip off my snuggies and unblanket my equines. When the thermometer in the barn registered twenty-two degrees, it felt positively balmy, and my glove liners and stocking cap made a crusty pile on the workbench. It was time, I decided, to remove the horses' heavy winter clothing and let them romp in the sun.

Leos Moneysink thought differently, and if looks could kill, I'd be next to the beheaded mouse on the doorstep right now. I reached for the front buckles of his State Line Tack Special forty-pound monster blanket, and he reached for my shoulder. We both backed off. I recognized—wisely—that my threat of exposing his butt to the cold was met with his counter-threat of exposing my skin to his teeth, and we both retreated to neutral corners. Maybe I was a bit hasty.

By mid-February, the weather really did seem to be about to break. No longer satisfied with merely the TV's Weather Channel for support, I watched like a hawk as the Weatherbug on my computer desktop blinked the temperature changes. The Weather Channel's Desktop Weather program popped open to remind me I had a responsibility to be informed at all times. My neighbor called to get confirmation. All signs pointed to a break in the Arctic Cold Front and a return—however brief—to full joint and muscle mobility. Yee-hah!

With the temperature approaching fifty, I ditched the insulated vest and three-season, weatherproof jacket in favor of less-bulky (and cleaner) couture, and off I went to the pasture. Leo was okay with being chosen this time. He didn't even seem to mind that my choice put him in harm's way as Zips Quirky Nutjob made a lunge for his neck on the way by. Pasture politics can be a rough game.

Recalling that my favorite horse psychic had just told me that Leo hated the static electricity discharge that came with blanket removal ("Snappy, snappy, snappy, he's telling me—it makes the lights go on"), I was careful to lift-and-toss rather than drag-and-flop the smelly hunk of Teflon-coated fiberfill. Not a single spark. I brushed him with equal caution, successfully avoiding the high-loft puffball effect in his long winter coat.

As I combed bits of hay from his tail, the moment of truth arrived. I spent another few minutes choosing exactly the right saddle pad, and handed over a bunch of peppermint horse cookies as a bribe before setting the saddle on his back, a helmet on my head, and his bit between my legs for warming. At that moment I realized that it wasn't Leo's mood I was concerned about. Leo is one of only two horses in my barn who can step over a sleeping fawn, launching the poor creature into terrified flight, and never even turn to watch it go. Leo makes faces and occasionally projects evil thoughts into the brains of the other horses, but he's my bombproof boy. A little static wasn't going to lessen his delight at the prospect of an outing after long weeks of standing around the water-cooler grousing about the weather with his co-workers. The sun was bright, the air warm, his belly was full of cookies, and all was right in Horse Land.

No, Leo wasn't the problem. I was. The weeks of layoff time probably hadn't done me any good. I'd filled them with weight-training at the gym—a new theory I was investigating in hopes of keeping some semblance of muscle tone during the time off—and had actually lost weight instead of layering winter fluff on my thighs and rear. Still, I looked out at the pasture, saw icy patches glinting in the sun, and wondered whether I'd be better off in the family room watching the Dr. Phil episodes I'd taped. Even if Leo was good as gold, even if my body was in perfect (if aging) condition, I'd be foregoing my customary warm-up in the ring and heading straight out into the open hayfield where deer-bogies and nightmare dogs could startle Leo into a disastrous shy. Ice hurts. Last year I'd landed on it on my head with remarkably good results in survival terms, but my butt hurt for days in sympathy.

The men-folk—my partner, Cliff, and my new farmhand, Cully—were cutting down dead trees along the pasture fence. I clung to the notion that, were I to make an unplanned vertical dismount, at least my remains wouldn't remain in the snow forever like a forgotten foolsicle. Another cookie for Leo (who struggled to chew it around the bit), and a deep breath for me, and together my trusty Quarter Horse and I marched down the driveway, heads high, orange drool speckling the snow.

I was still a little shaky as I lined my horse up with the mounting block. It wasn't until he did his usual butt-swing away from me, and we'd had our customary discussion about mounting block manners, that all the tension faded. Normalcy is a strong antidote to fear. I'm sure that's why prisoners-of-war are encouraged to replay golf games in their heads or try to recall the words to favorite songs. Keep it normal, and it doesn't matter whether or not it's real.

Leo and I had a good ride. We walked around the glittering hayfield, relaxing a little with each crunchy step. The ice proved to be mostly imaginary, but we were nonetheless careful not to incur its wrath. By the time we'd made the circuit and cut out onto the road, we were humming along like the old friends we were. Trotting up and down the driveway—the only clear place on the farm—we swung out with enthusiasm. Cars went by, deer and cows did what deer and cows do, and, stopping to get the mail from the box, we had a flawless time. All the work I'd put into keeping my muscles toned really had helped. My legs found their place with only a little testing, heels were down, back was relaxed, and hands were steady. Only the brain was short on control.

Every long layoff is a little scarier. Maybe it's my age, or maybe it's the number of lawn-dart moments I've accumulated over the years, but I always harbor the niggling fear that *this time* I won't be able to do it. *This time* I'll be too weak, too unbalanced, too old for one more season. Yet, every year I get better. Go figure.

Back in the pasture I turned Leo loose and made up to the others with hugs and pats for not choosing them all. The weather will get better, and they'll each have a turn, and with each ride I'll learn yet another little bit about what it means to ride. I'll probably never entirely lose the fear, but maybe, as the years go by, I'll spend less time grooming and more time riding. New beginnings, anyone?

All that glitters …

Chapter 6

Come Into the Light

As I've mentioned, spring came late this year. The winter was long and harsh, the horses miserable, the barn cold, my toes blue, everyone's mood nasty. Together, amid promises of green grass and sunshine, we awaited the coming warm weather. When it came, we were delirious. We ran and played, naked (the horses) and hairy (me). When, after a week, it went away again, beat to heck by an early-spring blizzard, we were beyond testy. How could this be? I checked to make sure my premium subscription to Weatherbug was paid up, and that this wasn't some nefarious tactic designed to lure me into renewing.

This is the sort of year that forces horse people to reassess their approach to the whole horse entanglement. Muffled by sarcasm, our enthusiasm for riding, regardless of discipline, takes on a dull, quiet urgency. Brilliant visions of challenge and progress are mired in reality, and if we have any resilience left at all, we think about finding ways around the problems. As awful as it might seem, this is prime time. It is only under stress that we leave the safe wallow of our accustomed routines and venture onto virgin turf.

The mucky, greasy ground was far from ideal for continued work with my fairly large, moderately attitudinal Paint gelding, Zip My Butt. We'd left off in the fall with him standing over me as I assessed the orthopedic damage quotient of his last tango with the Squirrel From Hell that inhabited the bushes surrounding the ring. Time may heal all wounds, but it does nothing for one's sense of confidence. By spring, that innocent pratfall had begun to loom large on my riding horizon, and Zip was not high on my list of preferred customers. Pokey Little Witch, Zip's mom, joined the roster of the officially retired as the mold spores drove her heaves into high gear, further limiting my options. So it was that I took a long look at my aging Quarter Horse, Leo.

This was a horse I'd bought some years ago from a boarder who'd lost solvency around the same time I lost my mind. She needed money; I needed another horse like I needed two more holes in my head. Bingo-bango, the deal was done. At the time, with my own two horses to ride and my collegiate daughter's three to exercise, there was little energy left for Leo. To a point, he was fine with this. Occasionally, however, he'd stand at the fence watching intently while I worked the other horses. He'd get in line and wait to be saddled. He'd walk into the grooming stall and stand between the cross-ties, hoping someone with a brush might wander by. His eyes followed my every move.

That first summer when Jess came home from college, I handed her the keys to her new school horse. She was not thrilled. Leo's previous owner had refused to let us lease the horse for her when she couldn't pay her board. Her reason? He was, in the vernacular, a nut job. His trustworthiness ranked somewhat lower than that of a local politician with designs on quitting his day job, she'd told me. She'd been asked repeatedly why she continued to own such a sideways animal, and she hadn't yet come up with a good answer other than that he was all she could afford. Jess looked askance at the pretty chestnut and asked me to accompany her to the ring for a test-drive. Just in case. Jess is a seasoned trainer, but hasn't had quite enough concussions yet to believe she doesn't need backup standing by on a first ride.

Leo had been with us for two years, and his owner had only ridden him a handful of times. When she had—only on her regular monthly board-paying visits—he'd become more and more difficult until, at last, she'd been unable to so much as walk him down the driveway without major histrionics (his) and abject terror (hers). Jess knew all of this and doubted my sanity. But, I knew Leo from the ground up. I'd been his caretaker, daily groomer, buddy and pal. There's something in the eye of a horse like Leo. Even while he's popping up and down in his best imitation of the Lone Ranger's Silver (Hi-*yo!* Away!), a horse like that has an eye that lets you know he's only kidding. He'll keep up the game until he loses, that eye says, or until you give up and go home. The key is to make sure he loses first.

Things did not look good for Leo during that first ride. He meandered around the ring, side-passing, running his chest into the gate with a loud *clang!*, and generally being as silly as a horse can be. At first glance, his movements appeared random, and Jess pronounced the horse unfit for anything but retirement. I asked her politely to just keep riding for a while, and she—she's a very good daughter at times—humored me. I was, after all, out a thousand dollars on this horse if we couldn't find a use for him.

Time passed, and since the horse hadn't done anything even slightly dangerous, she gave him a little leg towards a canter. That's when he came unglued. She stopped him and started again … and again … and again. She grew frustrated, and so did he. I began to wonder if this was such a great idea after all. We all took a breather.

Renewed, we tried again. She asked for a right-lead canter, and he missed. She stopped him. On the second try, he was visibly shaking. She asked; he missed again. By the third request, his eyes were rolling in his head. She asked; he reared … or so it appeared. Then, without further ado, they were cantering.

Leo's canter, in a word, sucked. It was choppy, short-strided, and he leaned inward seriously around the corners, giving rider and spectators the impression that the next step would topple him. In the weeks that followed, he did spend an inordinate amount of time on his knees as cornering got the better of him. But he tried. He tried very hard.

Time passed, and Jess finally found herself short a lesson horse. Much to his concern, Leo was conscripted. Every inch of him buzzed with curiosity as Jess and her young beginner student groomed and tacked him. He was anything but cooperative. Old as he is, he's still limber enough to swing his head around in the crossties and grab trouser on whoever is closest to his front end. We were learning a lot about this horse, and some of it made me cringe.

Once in the ring, Leo seemed possessed. He didn't misbehave in any classic way, but he immediately resumed the seemingly-random movements we'd seen before. The student aimed him down the rail, and he somehow wound up on the other side of the ring. She asked him to turn to the left, and he did, in a slow spin that left him facing the same direction. The look on his face was one of concentration, which threw us off. Was he trying to make a point?

Eventually the lesson ended, and Leo walked his rider to the barn, politely standing between the ties while she undressed and groomed him. Since he hadn't done anything really awful, Jess claimed him for her lesson program, and the deal was done.

The lesson ended, but the Leo story went on. With each passing week, Leo grew more confident in his new job. He stopped nipping during tack-up. He learned to tell time, and would head for the gate at precisely the stroke of 45-minutes. Despite his funky canter, he became a favorite among the beginners.

Leo's star had begun to shine, but it wouldn't reach full power for another year. It wasn't until my Paint pulled a stifle muscle leaving me short a horse that Leo really began to show his stuff. I hadn't ridden him much, so we began at the beginning: walk-trot-canter and small cross-rails done in kiddie-style two-point. With nothing better on the agenda, I opted to try to cure the inside lean. I set up barrels and cones, and we did a fine imitation of gymkhana for weeks. The ring took on a circus-like tone. Jumps with flowers and striped poles made a pattern around the outside, and cones and barrels took up the center. We'd work on the rail, do a few jumps, then hit the barrels. Leo loved it!

Within a month or so, I'd decided he was balanced enough to try a little dressage, so we did. Somewhere in Leo's past, someone did some nice work on his carriage and bending, and it all came back to him with little prompting. Before long we were "schooling" (as the show people say) Training Level. Not bad for Alpo.

Leo had his shining moment when, heart in my throat, I trailered him to a nearby cross-training facility for our first dressage test. It took him all of thirty seconds to acclimate to the new surroundings and sniff his way around the indoor arena, and we were ready. We did well. We did more than well. We won our first Intro Level test over Jess and her trainer and their well-schooled horses. We won! We scored in the mid-sixties, which, for my money, is as good as an eight-second barrel dash any day. The judge loved Leo almost as much as I did, complimenting his "workmanlike attitude" and his kind, devoted expression.

There is a moral to this long tale: You never know where you'll find a star rising in the darkness. Most horses, given a chance, will blind us with their kind-heartedness and their willingness to work with us in an honest and cooperative relationship. It's not the price tag that makes the horse; it's the tag that reads "Hello, My Name Is _____" and the mental handshake that comes with the first greeting. If you miss that, you may find yourself groping in the dark forever. Catch it, and you'll find yourself basking in unimaginable brightness. Moments pass and are lost, or their fleeting glitter feeds our dreams forever. I prefer glitter.

Chapter 7

▼

Left in the Lust

Finding oneself middle-aged is no small thing. Yesterday I was sixteen and praying I'd find a handsome boyfriend who would give me things and let me wear a Barbie wedding dress on my special day. At a recent Native American Pow Wow, I was dismayed to discover that I could no more mount the mechanical bull than I could play middle linebacker for the Cowboys. I have not been a happy camper since. In my head I was limber and lithe and grinning as the bull flung my flexible young body around. In my head I made an Olympic-quality dismount and landed with arms spread. My body, meanwhile, was looking for a seat in the shade where I could suck down my ice cream while younger bodies wobbled and shrieked on the back of the machine.

Be that as it may, this middle-aged thing bears closer scrutiny. Middle of what? Middle of the road? Middleweight? Certainly not middle of my life. I'm sure I've not come half-way through in such a short time as this. Heck! I still haven't worked up the nerve to tell my dad I don't think he looks good in plaid trousers!

The mechanical bull was surrounded by a throng of Britney Spears look-alikes. Not appreciating the contrast, I wandered over to the dance circle. The circle was alive with color and sound. Beautiful Native American women in "jingle" dresses and men decked out in turkey and eagle feathers hopped and stepped to the tune of drums and chanting. I gave the entire experience a "9" on a scale of 10. It had a good beat. I could have danced to it if I hadn't been sunk in the mire of my newly-acquired stigma.

How does all this apply to my horse life? Well, standing in my field at the time was a lovely mare, a Thoroughbred with gaits like silk and the conformation of a calendar horse. This mare was and is my daughter's, and she's chronically for sale. My daughter, far wiser than I, recognized that at twenty-five and soon to be married, she needed to cut down on the excitement in her life and take a more realistic approach. She talked at length about the "packer" she would buy with the proceeds from the sale of the pretty mare.

I, being much older and, therefore, not nearly so wise, lusted after that mare. I wanted to be the one slipping lithely onto her back and riding those amazing, silky strides and jumping those huge (to me) jumps with flair and abandon. My daughter offered me the horse for below her public asking price, which rendered the mare quite inexpensive compared to other horses I've seen with less talent and far coarser looks.

At last, I could take it no more. Checkbook in hand, I strode confidently to the barn and asked permission to ride the mare. Jess was fine with that. "Ride her whenever you like," she said magnanimously. "She can use the exercise, and I'd rather ride The Rat any day." Grinning, she turned on her heel and went in search of the little Morgan who is her alter ego.

Dolly is a wonderful horse in many ways. She is absolutely sane from the ground. I can do whatever I wish to her, around her, above and below her, and she will stand without moving. She loves to be scratched and have her udder rubbed, and will stand ground-tied outside the tack room door waiting for cookies at the end of a ride. She does hate to be caught in the main pasture, but in a smaller area, she comes when called. She's been John-Lyons-ed into a coma. I brushed and polished and hugged and fussed over her until we both sighed with pleasure. I tacked her up then, and off we went to the ring.

I'd ridden Dolly before, many times, but not recently. While Jess was at college, I'd even taken the mare to the back field under western tack and run barrels with her for a bit. We got along perfectly. I had great faith that she would remember me with fondness and give me the wonderful, electric (but safe) ride I was craving.

Maybe it was my imagination, but as my butt hit the saddle and she began to tap-dance, she seemed a bit *too* electric. Off we went around the ring at a walk, and my initial skepticism was replaced by calm as she stretched her neck and back and sighed. I smiled. She snorted. I put some leg on her and urged her into a lovely extended trot. She obliged.

By this time, Jess was at the fence on the "Mommy Bench" watching us, The Rat grazing at the end of a lead. She shouted a couple of instructions, which I followed. Dolly got rounder and more collected, and my heart sang.

"Push her into the canter," she called. "Slow and easy; don't squeeze; just think 'canter', and she'll go."

Yeah. Well, before the thought had even budded in my brain, Dolly plucked it and ran with it. She wasn't running away, she was just cantering, those athletic, balanced strides I so envied unrolling under me. I should have had a Nirvana Moment at that point, but I didn't. She's a long-strided horse, and she reached the corner before I was balanced for the turn. No, she didn't dump me. We continued around the ring, but she was listing to the left, and I was hanging onto her mane with one hand, trying not to lean with her and knock her down.

A few strides later I brought her to a trot, then a walk, and at last I breathed. What was that all about? Where was my leg? How could I have reached the terror threshold so quickly when all we were doing was cantering along the familiar fence line? This, I concluded, was middle-age pounding me between the shoulder blades and saying, "Heigh-di-ho, Woman! Welcome to the downhill slide!"

I'm better now. It's taken months of visits to the gym for me to jam my body back into some sort of condition for riding. I'd gotten lazy was what had happened. I'd gotten cocky, too. Forty-plus years in the saddle does not a rider make, I found out. It had been two years since my last challenging ride, and it showed.

The question became, then, where would I go with this? I could buy the beautiful mare and hope that eventually my heart would sink back down out of my throat to its proper spot in my chest, or I could admit that perhaps my young Paint gelding was challenge enough at this stage of my life. I chose the latter. The lust remains, but it is tempered by a certainty that I no longer have it in me to push the envelope. Hell! I'm lucky if I can muster enough spit to glue it shut! I've still got horses to ride, and there are exciting moments, but I became content to replace Jess on the Mommy Bench and watch from the sidelines as other, extraordinarily limber young Dressage-Queens-in-training came to try the pretty mare's flowing gaits. I'll pack my aging Quarter Horse, Leos Big Butt, into the trailer and head to my trainer's for another lesson, and I'll be as stiff and sore as I need to be after an hour of "bring that shoulder *up,* not *out!*" Like the bodies waving from the back of the mechanical bull and the handsome young men waiting to catch them when they fall, the mare will take her place on the Who Are You Kidding list. We'll both be better off that way.

A match made in Heaven can take years of hell to achieve.

CHAPTER 8

Buyers and Sellers

Buying and selling horses has never been easier or more efficient. No longer do buyers have to stand for hours in the hot sun while a dealer parades a selection of equines before him for his consideration. No longer does the locating of exactly the right horse depend on sheer luck. With the advent of Internet trading, the horse business has taken a sharp leap into the twenty-first century, and the ramifications are truly awesome.

First, rest assured that the private treaty sale between friends is still alive and well, and the tack shop and feed store walls are still papered with hand-made posters offering horses for sale or begging for someone to turn loose a perfect partner at a reasonable price before the next show season. But those means of horse trading are becoming the dinosaurs of the horse world. Online shopping has trumped in-person schlepping, which is not a bad thing by any means. Point-and-click has found a perfect niche among busy horsemen as an effective and efficient way of trading.

Here's how it works:

You've got a horse to sell. Maybe you're a dealer with several horses, or maybe you finally realized that at 13 hands, My Friend Fuzzbutt just isn't going to cut it as a jumper. You go online and post ads at websites like Dreamhorse.com, Horsecity.com, Freehorseads.com, and the granddaddy of them all, boasting over 50,000 listings at any given time, Equine.com. There are dozens of sites willing to help you unload Fuzzbutt and make room for your new horse, often with free advertising space, so you pick one and give it a shot. You post your ad, and you wait for the perfect buyer (or the first patsy, depending on where you stand on the horse seller continuum) to email or call so that you can pack your animal off to a new home with as little fuss and bother as possible.

You want to buy a horse. You go online and read the ads at websites like Equine.com et al. You email and call and make arrangements to visit a dozen horses in a dozen days. You print out the photographs supplied by the sellers and tape them to the wall or stack them on your desk. Everyone who visits is forced to look at the pictures and give an opinion. Your Aunt Elaine finally calls to say, "I'm not coming over if you're going to make me look at horse pictures again. I'll just toss your birthday gift out of the car window onto the driveway."

Eventually seller and buyer find each other in the great mating game that is the Internet, and a miracle happens. The buyer happily loads his new child into a trailer and heads for home, while the seller hustles to the bank to make sure the check will clear. A fine time has been had by all. A process that might have taken months a few short years ago now takes days. A boon indeed for horse owners who also have jobs where their presence is required, and "I've got to see a man about a horse" is not considered a viable excuse for absence.

So what's so special about horse shopping online?

1. The assortment of horses available is astounding. A recent shopping foray uncovered horses within a mile or two of my farm at stables I didn't know existed. I wouldn't have known to call them because I'd never heard of them. These are horses that might be perfect for my needs, and many might otherwise have wound up languishing or going to auction while the sellers sat hoping someone would see their poster at the supermarket and call.

2. The search engines used by some of the sites are so efficient it's possible to narrow down your shopping to a specific breed trained to a particular level in a certain discipline. Like seeing that special dress at Nordstrom.com, clicking the size, color and availability menus and hitting a match, finding exactly the horse you're looking for is a heady experience.

3. Prices appear to be dropping. This may be a function of the current economic environment, but the Internet is also having an impact. My last horse-shopping experience led me to the big, well-known and advertised horse malls nearby. Prices were high, mainly because these dealers knew they were the only show in town. At least they were the only ones readily available to the general horse public. Choices were few, which meant the opportunity for a bad decision was ripe. This time around, those same dealers are listing their horses on the websites with the Average Joe horse owners, some of whom have very nice horses indeed for sale at a reasonable price. Competition will always result in lower prices.

4. The details are available right up front. Not that there isn't a certain charm to sitting in a horse trader's office flipping through pages of registration papers looking for just the line you're interested in. The social value of those hours mustn't be overlooked. To click a link, however, and have photos, detailed descriptions, and pedigrees appear is a great time-saver. It even makes it possible to check with the breed association to make sure the horse described and pictured is actually registered under that name and to those owners. The days of shady paper-trading may well be over.

5. You still get to look at and try the horses. This is where the real fun is, and the new process makes it easier to reach this point. Once you have found a few likely prospects, all of the websites have forms which can be used to send reasonably well-protected emails to the owners. You can ask questions, ask for more photos,

and, if it seems wise, set up an appointment to meet and ride the horse.

This all sounds almost too good to be true, and to a point it is. On the seller's end, there is a distinct down side in the form of tire-kickers. Every seller has come across the erstwhile buyer who is, in truth, making the rounds, trying out different horses just because it's fun to do. They're hard to screen for. Time wasted showing a horse to someone who has no intention of buying it is never worthwhile, and has been the bane of horse sellers' jobs for centuries. With the ads so plainly available to the public, the number of wannabees has also increased. Every seller I contacted during my recent search made at least one remark about another buyer who had been a waste of time in a busy schedule, testing the water to see if I might also be that type.

On the buyer's end, sometimes the horse is not exactly as described. Sometimes it's barely recognizable. I only found one instance when the animal in question was nothing like the description in the ad, but I only searched for a couple of weeks and only visited six horses before making my decision.

Still, that beat my previous experiences when I looked at an average of two horses before buying the one that was less lame or more likely to live through the trailering home. Many of my equines fell into my barn led strictly by the hand of fate. That's not likely to happen again with the Web to help me shop.

It's possible to project the impact of this process into the future of the horse business. If buyers have more products available, they will be pickier about price and quality. This should, in the long run, mean more reasonable prices and more attention to breeding. While the long-backed, ewe-necked Quarter Horse cross (crossed, presumably, with an elk) was adorable, the papered gelding with the rack of blue ribbons for nearly the same price was an obvious winner. Perhaps the Internet will be the answer to the problem of bad backyard breedings that has plagued the horse world for decades. Susie is less likely to decide to breed that knock-kneed, attitudinal, mixed-breed mare nibbling turnip tops in her vegetable garden if she realizes that the baby won't be worth squat on the open market. Even her friends won't be tempted to buy it when they can compare and contrast so effectively with better-bred babies just a few blocks away.

What do buyers want? My research shows that they want a decent horse, a fair price, and no deceit. They want to shop for horses like they shop for cars. One day there will be a site that will offer the 360-degree rotating holographic view of the horse in motion that all tech-savvy buyers crave. For now, at least there is more information than ever before available to the discerning shopper. No longer does the purchase of a horse have to depend entirely on the split-second bond that occurs when you stand in a paddock and make eye contact with some scruffy, down-in-the-mouth retired school horse. This is a major boon to those of us who are completely emotional horse buyers. We're protected for at least a few moments from our own foolishness.

A word to the wise, though, should be inserted here. There are a *lot* of really nice horses out there. The temptation to keep looking until we find the Perfect Companion can be overwhelming. With such a wide field from which to choose, decision-making becomes more difficult. Set yourself a limit (or several), and stick to it, or you will still be looking at horses two years down the road.

What do sellers want? Honest buyers. Don't waste a seller's time by looking at horses you don't intend to buy. Don't shop outside your price range in hopes of talking the seller down. Don't look at horses that are far too advanced for your level of riding or that are not trained in the discipline you intend to pursue. You can talk all day, but fourth level dressager, Wispy Will, isn't going to become a barrel horse just because you wish it so. Why torment everyone involved? Why risk life and limb to hop aboard a 1200-pound jumper when you know the best you've ever done was a short walk on your daughter's lead-line pony or an hour's hack on a stringer at a resort hotel? Sellers want the sale to go smoothly, free of silliness and follow-up lawsuits.

The Internet has raised the bar for horse trading. Relax and go find yourself a horse or sell the one you've got. It's a whole new world out there, and it's a lot more fun than the old one!

Chapter 9

▼

Dumb Human Tricks 101

My horse, Zip, forgave me today. Which of my many transgressions of herd law had caused him to stop speaking to me for four days, I can only guess. For a herd leader, I'm pretty stupid and not very trainable, and Zip takes my idiocy very personally. My punishment, as always, was ostracism. When he's irritated with me, he simply cuts me out of the herd. He stops speaking to me in a way that is typically equine and easy for a human—particularly one with my obvious learning disability—to misinterpret because it doesn't look the same in each horse.

Understanding herd law is a lot like trying to take a calculus test in a foreign language. Just when you think you've got the whole thing figured out, you, in your infernally annoying human way, make eye contact with the wrong horse at the wrong time, and you're back in the doghouse wondering what went wrong. That's if you're lucky. A really numb human may miss the fact that Magic Mayhem isn't speaking to him, forcing the horse to escalate to kicking, biting, bucking, and generally causing as much physical pain as is necessary to get his human's attention—the equine version of shouting.

So, four days ago, I did something horrible. I honestly didn't mean it. Another, less emotional horse would have let me slide, but Zip, like his mother, feels the need to communicate his every mood. What I did, as far as I can figure, was cross the boundaries of decency by choosing to ride another, lower-status gelding when Zip came up lame for his workout. He would have been fine with my saddling his mom or the herd boss. In fact, anyone above him in status would have been a fine choice in his eyes. He would have been able to hold his head up in herd social settings and explain generously that "Poor human. Well, I guess if she can't have me, she doesn't mind settling for Super Dude."

But the horse I chose was just a shade below Zip in herd standings. This was a gelding who was a relative late-comer to the herd, and one Zip had beaten up successfully on many occasions. That he's ten years older than Zip doesn't matter. Leo is only a few bite marks above the one-eyed boarder horse, low man on the totem pole for the entire ten years he's been with the herd. This was, I must assume, a slap in the muzzle to Zip.

The cause, then, is reasonably obvious. The effect of my foolish choice is a little more subtle. In post-mortem analysis, I note the following:

1. When I doctored Zip's sore leg and turned him out, he was in fine spirits.

2. When I took Leo out of the pasture and led him to the barn, Zip was still smiling.

3. When I reappeared with the saddled Leo, Zip was pointedly ignoring us.

4. When I mounted and began the ride, Zip stopped eating long enough to give us a quick once-over.

5. When the workout started in earnest, and I loudly praised Leo for his perfect attention, Zip stopped eating and came to the fence to watch.

6. When I finished the hard work of dressage and jumping and switched to Play Time in the form of a few rounds of barrel racing, Zip's face hung over the fence within nipping range.

7. When I un-tacked and lead Leo to the lawn for a hand-grazing reward period, Zip's expression changed to something between forlorn and irritated.

8. When I turned Leo out with the herd, Zip immediately approached him, sniffed him once, then bit him on the butt.

Now, I've never bitten another woman, but I've certainly felt the urge. I can clearly remember the time my ex-ed spouse showed up at the barn with his new flame. Biting, sadly, was out of the question. If I could have, I would have, but I couldn't, so I didn't. Zip, on the other hand, felt no such human compunctions, and Leo sported the tell-tale "I Cheated With Your Owner and Paid the Price" mark for a few days.

How did Leo take all of this? Oddly, he was fine with it. In the post-ride afterglow, all he wanted was hugs and nose-snurffles, and Zip's threatening glares got no rise out of him. Could he have been flaunting his transgression just a bit, rubbing Zip's muzzle in it with some pointed equine body language? I'd say that's another safe bet. Given the fact that Leo became my shadow for a few days following the event, while Zip did his best to crawl into my lap at every opportunity, I'm going to guess that there was a change in herd dynamics afoot. I was the witless (read: Stupid Human) catalyst.

If hostilities had escalated, I might have needed to step in and change things again. In fact, I did make a point of taking Zip out to graze after my sessions with Leo until Zip's leg healed enough for him to be put back into the lineup. In the meanwhile, Zip's mom, Pokey, also feeling a bit left out, took to standing at the gate staring at me, beaming "take me next" clearly into my brain, so she got her licks in, too.

All of that is very interesting, but there was something else that niggled at the back of my sorry human brain. There are seven horses in my herd. I am the Major Player in their care and feeding, and I brush each of them daily and have lovely chats with them all to make sure no one feels left out. I have done dressage with Rat and played at barrels with Dolly; Grady and I had pleasant trail rides before his retirement, and I'm the only one who fusses over the boarder horse, Pinky, while Pokey, who is chronically lame, rarely is ridden at all. So, how is it that only the three horses I actually own felt the need to vie for my attention during that period? How do they figure out the ownership issue?

Twice in my experience I've seen owners chosen by horses who were not actually theirs. It happened once at a boarding farm when a mare, sold to a new owner, made her choice of the barn owner's husband quite obvious. She simply bit the new owner on the shoulder hard enough to draw blood, then, like a lover with a proclivity for S&M, faked a kick at her chosen owner's head, indicating clearly, "I'm *not* to be sold, you idiot! Now get over here and hug me."

The second time was when the ranch horse my daughter had bought to use for lessons tried his darnedest to kill everyone around him *except* for the dealer who was supposed to be selling him for us. He made his ownership preferences clear enough so the dealer bought him, and they rode into the sunset, happy as piss clams at high tide.

Now, I'm not suggesting we buy horses by standing in the pen at the sale barn and waiting for one to approach and ask for our hand in marriage, nor am I saying that a rider should chose her mount based on how offended the other horses might be by her choice. What I am saying is that it never hurts to be a little diplomatic when you're messing with a bunch of animals that outweigh the entire Packers' defense. There are times when it just doesn't pay to be too human. Whether or not you understand which law you've broken is unimportant. Just swallow your pride and pay the fine. Even if you don't fake understanding horse language very well, they'll love you for the effort.

Chapter 10

The Five Horses We Meet on Earth

You may only become intimate with one horse in your lifetime, but you'd be the exception rather than the rule. Once the horse hair gets in your blood, there's no stopping you. Maybe you'll only own one horse, but other horses will sense the kinship in you (or perhaps it's just the eau de manure on your boots that makes them want to get to know you) and work their way into your sphere of reality, invited or not. There are even horses you'll never meet who will have an effect on you. You simply can't have just one.

Like the five pivotal people in your life, the horses will change you in subtle ways—some good, some bad, some just different—and it will be up to you to decide what you will do with the changes.

1. The Intro Horse. We each came to horses in our own way, but it was always with a horse leading us. This might have been a friend's first pony, or perhaps it was an old draft horse on a farm you once visited. It might have been a real-life meeting, or an imaginary one. I was escorted to the party by The Black, Walter Farley's star horse in the *Black Stallion* series. I don't remember how I got the first book, but I remember well saving my allowance to buy the rest at the local bookstore. The series was new-born, and each additional title sent me into paroxysms of delight. I drew pictures of The Black and his boy, Alec Ramsey. I dreamed about them, wrote about them in my diary, and imagined that one day I would have an adventure that would rival anything that Farley could dream up.

I never made it to Arabia, but I have had my fair share of adventures over the years. Without that big black horse, I might never have developed the obsession that would eventually take over my life, leaving me drool-stained and stinky, but glorious in my dementia.

When you think back, you will find a single horse at the heart of your own horselife. If you're female—as 80% of all horse people are—it didn't take much to trigger the elemental connection and launch you into oblivious horse lust. If you're a guy, odds are you were talked into trying the horse thing by a female. It doesn't matter; there was still a first horse present at the induction ceremony. From that horse, all your subsequent experiences sprang, and he colored your view of horses permanently.

2. The Experimental Horse. Once you had crossed the line between "Damn, they're big!" and "Wow! Can I try that?" you found yourself face-to-face with the horse that would suffer through your early attempts at figuring out the whole horse experience. This horse probably didn't belong to you. It might have been a lesson horse at a training facility or a hack horse on a bedraggled line at a resort somewhere. Perhaps you had a friend who had a horse she was willing to let you try your hand with. Wherever this horse came from, he probably didn't benefit from the encounter as much as you did.

My Experiment was a Pinto lesson horse named Maverick. He was from "Out West", wherever that was. He wasn't my first lesson horse, but he was the one I felt the need to really try to ride. Before I met Maverick, I'd been a passenger. Granted, I had a certain style despite the poofy, early-Sixties breeches, but with a bunch of lessons under my belt, I still really hadn't a clue what I was doing. Maverick made me work for everything he gave me. He made me wear my helmet, too, after the time I lost my grip after a cross-rail experience and was forced into a novel, crablike position under his belly until he lost interest in my presence and stopped for lunch. He jumped like a rabbit—with all four feet together—making it hard enough to stay on him, but he didn't have any meanness in him. Mean Experiment horses generally wind up ending a person's desire to join the ranks of horsemen. Maverick was just high-spirited. Very high-spirited.

From Maverick I learned that there was more to this whole riding thing than just keeping my back straight and my heels down, so I guess the experiment was a success. If you're reading this book, odds are your Experiment was also successful. Congratulations! You experimented yourself out of sanity and right into poverty and helmet hair.

3. The Connected Horse. For horses and humans to work together without bloodshed, there has to be a connection. The first horses we meet don't really connect with us, nor do we with them. Those are experiences in survival and tests of endurance. The Connected Horse is the first horse you truly bond with. This is the horse that sounds a chord that lives so deep in you that you might never have heard it otherwise. One horse comes into your life and turns your hobby into a passion. Suddenly you are aware of horses as sentient, feeling creatures not so unlike yourself, and you are amazed by them For me, this enlightenment came in the form of an aging Quarter Horse mare named Fancy who was my alter-ego and best friend and who still, ten years post-mortem, grazes the green pastures of my dreams.

The down side to the relationship you form with this horse is that eventually it will end. Horses get old and die, just like people. People run out of money or time or energy and sell horses. Horses are outgrown. However this special bond ends, it is one you will remember for the rest of your life. The Connector is the irreplaceable horse you will still be reminiscing about when you are drooling into your oatmeal at the Home. Horse folks have been known to spend fortunes trying to recreate that relationship, but it can't be done.

The Connector not only teaches you about horses, he also teaches you about connecting with other people. For a dumb animal, he has a huge and very important role to play in your life. He will mature you and make you a better person, while he teaches you about a sport that requires as accessories a fat wallet, thick skin, and an understanding family. You'll discover the real meaning of "live and learn".

4. The Challenger. Into each horseperson's life a little challenge must fall. Eventually you will lose a large number of brain cells due to age, exposure to manure fumes, or friendship with a horse person even crazier than you are. It's a Law of Nature; don't try to fight it. You'll know you've reached the stage where The Challenger will enter your life when you stop ducking into the tack room when Loopy Louise is lead into the barn by her electric witch-mare, Horrorfest. You'll have read that one final training book, bought yourself a clicker and a heading rope, and there you'll stand, arms crossed, assessing the situation as if you actually knew what the situation was. You'll hear a voice that sounds suspiciously like yours say, "Need some help with that mare?"

Before you can slap yourself silly, Louise will have tearfully handed you the lead, and you will have crossed the threshold with The Challenger. It might be difficult to believe, as you are flying down the aisle way on the losing end of a braided cotton line, but you actually need this horse in your life. You may even offer Louise money for the privilege of taking over the ownership and training of the horse that has been striking fear in the hearts of trainers and riders for a decade. Louise is on her way to meet the last of her Five Horses, and she'll happily pass on her Challenger to someone who is obviously ready to move to the next level.

Oddly, you may find this to be the perfect horse for you ... for now. You will spend months—or years—trying out training tips on your Challenger horse. You will spend a fortune on equipment and learn more than you would have imagined about what to do with it all. You'll forge new friendships as your farrier, vet and assorted friends and orthopedic surgeons will be happy to discuss with you your progress, or lack thereof. This will be a huge learning experience. Other horses will come and go from your life, but none will teach you as much as fast as this one.

For me, the Challenger came in the form of a baby born to a mare I'd bought pregnant. The entire situation was part of the challenge, and I got there thanks to a rabid horse person who had me in her thrall. In one great swoop I learned about the care of pregnant mares, how to deal with founder, how to birth a baby, and how to survive the rigors of saddle-breaking (which I did *not* do myself) and training a youngster. This was a crash course, and there were many moments along the way when I wondered if I should just pack it in and buy a bicycle while I still had some bones left intact.

Survival is key. So are good health insurance and a job which allows you ample time off for recuperation. Put into proper perspective, while the Challenger might well damage you, physically and emotionally, beyond all repair, without this horse, you will never realize your potential as a horse person or even as a human being. Look past the fractures, sprains and bloody gashes, and you will see a tough side of yourself you never would have encountered. Once you have mastered creating a working relationship with a horse with "issues", you will never again worry about what anyone thinks of you in any area of your life. You will be wearing an invisible, bulletproof "Because I'm the Mommy, *That's* Why!" t-shirt. The benefits of having met The Challenger will serve you for life, even if common sense kicked in after a week, and you sold him to the guy who swears he can break a mustang by singing John Denver songs. You will find strength in whatever decision you make, and you will have overcome fears you didn't know you had.

5. Your Deepest Heart. There will come a time when you will look at yourself with a cold, appraising eye, and you'll have to be honest about your continued ability to deal with The Challenger and other difficult horses. At that point, you'll seek out the horse that will be your soul mate forever. By the time you have met this horse, you will know everything you're going to learn about horse training. You will have owned and sold all the fancy equipment and trendy tack you'll ever need. You might have a backyard big enough to keep this horse, in which case you will become inseparable buddies. At the very least, you will find a nearby farm where you will board this wonderful animal until either the horse dies or you do. This will be your last horse in every sense.

There's a good chance this horse might be a retired show horse or an off-the-track adoptee. In all likelihood, your Heart-Horse will not be a youngster. When you have reached the stage of wanting nothing more than to love and bond with a peaceful, sane animal, you will probably have also recognized that your age is such that a young horse might well outlive you … or at least your useful riding years. You will choose, then, an animal who speaks to your spirit without challenging you physically.

You'll know when you've found your Heart-Horse. You'll find yourself spending more and more time at the barn just hanging out with your horse, grazing him on the lawn, grooming him to a shine, talking over your day. You might not clip his muzzle, though you'll keep his bridle path clear for the occasional comfy trail ride or slow hour of work in the ring. You'll have bought him the most comfortable, best-fitting second-hand equipment because neither of you was in the mood to break in something hard and unforgiving. Maybe you'll still go to shows and ride—brilliantly or barely—in the Alzheimer's class. Maybe you'll just stay home. Whatever you do, one day you'll realize that after all the money you spent on animal communicators and trainers, you only had to stop and listen and you would have clearly heard your horse's thoughts and desires. Together you'll stand and stare into the distance, watching the days recede.

One day your Heart-Horse will tell you his final secret, and you'll help him to that place where he can rest with the very best of your memories. You'll bury him in peace, keeping his halter and a lock of braided tail hair to hang on the garage wall, and you won't buy another horse. Your memories will remain as precious to you as anything money can buy, and you'll know in your heart that you'll see this last horse friend again one day soon. As you spend your days leafing through the mental scrapbook of your horse life, your Heart-Horse will be looking over your shoulder.

As luck will have it, sometimes the horses come to you in the wrong order. You'll know when you've lost the way, because you'll think about quitting horses altogether. Should that happen, don't try to retrace your steps. Look for the Heart-Horse and go straight into his world. You'll know that you've missed a little, but you've had the best.

The Experimental Horse

The Connected Horse

Chapter 11

Little Big Horse

Duke's arrival was greeted with mixed reactions. To wit:

"Did I see something tiny in the front paddock, or am I hallucinating again?"

"You bought *what?*"

"Uh … cute. What can he do beside eat?"

"Aren't you afraid the other horses will roll on him and kill him?"

"*Ooooo!* I want one!"

This was to be expected. A week after the fact, as all 34.5 inches of miniature stallion Lazy A Blue Mist grazed peacefully alongside sixteen-hand Zip, I was a bit taken aback myself. Such are the whims of horse people. In my ongoing search for a suitable trail horse for my partner and other random friends, I'd left the farm to look at a fifteen-hand Quarter Horse gelding and returned with an eight-hand stud. No one ever said horse people follow the beaten path.

The desire to own a "mini" had lurked in my head for quite some time before Duke popped up in an online ad. I'd read about mini therapy and seeing-eye horses, and I'd gushed over the tiny equines in their minuscule harnesses pulling carts full of normal-sized people at the state fair. With age comes a certain desire to tone it down a notch, so the prospect of owning a horse small enough for me to push around without danger of being stomped to death was appealing. I'd clicked on the ad by accident, and by week's end, Duke was in my barnyard chasing the big geldings and loving up the fifteen-two Paint mare.

Naturally a bit of research, in books, online and on the ground, was in order. I learned the following:

- None of the books in my library believes in miniature horses. Not even *The Complete Book of Horses.* Not so complete, I'd say.
- Miniature horses are not a kind of pony.
- Minis may have originally been bred, like Shetland ponies, to work in the mines, hauling the ore carts. In any case, they've been around for roughly 400 years, which is plenty long enough to qualify them as a breed, not just a mutation.
- There are two registries: American Miniature Horse Association (AMHA) and American Miniature Horse Registry (AMHR). In 1976 AMHR, a subdivision of the American Shetland Pony Club (founded 1888), was created. The club accepts two classes of minis: A and B. Division A minis are under 34 inches in height. Division B is over 34 inches. AMHA, founded in 1978, requires that "breed standard" horses stand no taller than 34 inches at the last hairs on the withers. There's some rivalry between AMHR and AMHA members, but I'm not clear on the source.
- Miniature horses are not shrunk-down versions of big horses or ponies, though they are identical to their full-sized brethren in conformation.

- The mini is sometimes used as a seeing-eye horse or a companion horse for elderly or disabled persons.
- They come in all kinds of shapes and colors, from draft to Arabian, heavy to refined, basic black to parti-colored. There's a mini for every taste!
- Miniature horse foals are incredibly small. Imagine a German short-haired pointer puppy with hooves.
- You can ride a mini. More precisely, your 30 to 50-pound grandchild can. Don't buy one if riding him yourself is your goal.
- Minis make great driving horses. They are personable and amenable to training and can pull loads up to 400 pounds, which is respectable. They require special carts that are custom-balanced to take the stress off the horses' little legs and backs.
- You can get little rubber booties for them if you have the urge to take them indoors for some reason. Nursing home visits come to mind. So do bachelor parties, but let's put a big negative stamp on that idea.
- They don't eat much. They have little stomachs. That leaves them plenty of time to find ways out of the pasture or harass the big horses in your herd.
- A mini stallion is just like a big stallion, so don't get cocky. They can bite your butt and kick your kneecaps out if you get careless.
- They're just so darned *cute*!

Not one to take too many chances, I hedged my bet by checking with a mini-owning friend who agreed to help me find Duke a new home if things didn't work out. As it turned out, my fear that he would be injured by one of his new herd mates was far from the reality.

Duke and I arrived at the farm in mid-afternoon. I planned it that way so that there would be plenty of daylight left for me to assess his behavior and introduce him to the first of the big horses he would meet. My three-board slip rail fence was a bit of a concern. I was worried that if the mini put his mind to it, he could easily slide the center board and hop to freedom before I could grab him. The round pen adjoining the barnyard, however, has five-foot high tubular steel panels with little space between the rails. I checked it for dangerous objects, hung a water bucket, and turned Duke loose. The pen was larger than the paddock in which he'd been living, and he sped around, bucking and squealing, investigating every inch of the space. There was grass galore as the pen hadn't been getting much use. He was in hog heaven.

To that point, Duke's experience with full-sized horses had been limited to a pinto pony that lived with three minis at Duke's former home. The first horse I chose to introduce to Duke was Pinky the One-Eyed Wonder App. He's low man on the herd roster, mostly because there's not an aggressive gene in him. I figured he'd be least likely to seem threatening to the newcomer. The two sniffed through the bars, Pinky faked a few charges at the gate (which Duke ignored completely), and by supper they were grazing on opposite sides of the rails in peace.

Over a period of a week I worked Duke up through the herd hierarchy. For a short horse, he has a very tall attitude. There was a little squealing and fussing when he met Leo, the aging Quarter Horse gelding, then they settled their differences and buddied up. Zip, second in herd order, was easy. He's a lover, not a fighter, so I felt confident throwing him into the larger paddock with Duke and Leo for a day. No problem. Later I had a second-thought moment when I noticed that Duke's halter and fly hat made a great handle for mini-tossing, and Zip was enjoying the game immensely. Duke wised up quickly, learned to duck, and peace was restored.

The Paint mare went into heat instantly, so she would be the last horse the mini stud would meet. Eventually she went of season, and I didn't have to worry that she might pee on his head and drown him.

The challenge proved to be the oldest horse and herd leader, Grady. There was a lot of hostility between the two from the get-go. If looks could kill . .! I worried that Grady would pick up Duke and fling him, stomping him to death when he landed. As it turned out, that was, indeed, the plan. Neither of us counted on Duke's big-boy attitude.

Loose in the barnyard together for the first time, their supervised play seemed to go remarkably well—well enough, in fact, for me to decide to leave them alone after an hour or so. I hadn't been gone for more than five minutes when I heard all hell break loose. The squealing and screaming cost me at least a hundred new grey hairs. Visions of bloody little bodies flashed through my head. I couldn't have been farther off base.

I rounded the corner, and into sight popped Grady running hell-bent down the long side of the barnyard. He made the turn at the corner, and I saw Duke, neck snaked to the ground, not more than two feet behind Grady and going flat-out. There was a scrape down Duke's back where Grady had tried unsuccessfully to muscle him into submissiveness. They disappeared behind the barn, as I hopped the fence. As they came flying up the long side again, I grabbed Duke by the halter (praise the mini for being light enough for an old lady to stop with one hand!), and marched him to the round pen. Grady was huffing and puffing, feeling, I'm sure, every one of his twenty-six years.

Things grew considerably more settled over time. There were still issues between Duke and Grady requiring permanent separation, but the energy seemed to be draining out of the conflict. Eventually Grady succumbed to cancer and old age, and peace reigned in the barnyard once again.

So, I address the next question, which is what to do with the little guy. Feeding and petting are fine. Mini horses make mini manure, so clean-up is a breeze. There are plenty of hours left in the day for fun and games.

Enter credit cards and online shopping!

Be aware that you can't go to the corner tack shop and buy stuff for a miniature horse. Some items in "foal" size—halters and the occasional sheet or blanket—will fit a Division A mini or a B with a small head or short body. For the most part, nothing in a big-horse store will do for a little horse, so you're in for a truly exciting shopping experience.

There are quite a few online resources. A www.dogpile.com search for "miniature horse tack", "miniature horse blankets", and simply "miniature horse" turned up several suppliers of mini goods. Minis are easy to handle, so they're easy to measure. I highly recommend that you take a full set of measurements all at once, because absolutely nothing about minis is standardized. You'll be meeting lots of nice folks as you email measurements and questions back and forth.

EBay proved to be a fine source for inexpensive driving harnesses, so that's where I started. Within a couple of days I had won what looked like a fairly decent starter outfit for around $100. There were used harnesses available cheaper, and nylon ones, but I feel safest with new leather. I've made too many unplanned full-frontal landings due to faulty equipment to continue taking chances.

Unfortunately, no one had any other mini equipment up for auction that week, so I was forced to strike out on my own. I needed a bit to go with the harness, and I found one at State Line Tack. They carry a very limited line of mini stuff. Lucky for me bits were on the list.

From there I went back to dogpile.com to search for "easy-entry" carts. My little guy was green-broke to drive. I'd already tried him before I bought him and knew he would be fine, but I didn't want to spend big bucks on a fancy show-quality cart prematurely. There are lots of carriage makers who produce items in mini size. There's an equally wide variety of prices. From the cheapest easy-entry cart at $350 plus shipping, prices rose gradually until reaching a high of well over $7000 for a "Cinderella's Pumpkin", multi-mini-hitch carriage made for pony parties and other celebratory events. The optional hitch tongue on that one cost as much as the entire low-end easy-entry cart.

I picked a middle-range custom-built easy-entry cart with a couple of options ("spares" box, brass whip holder) and sent off a check for $315, a half-price down-payment.

A winter blanket is a must in the Northeast, so I found a place that had those. A training surcingle turned up on eBay, and the side reins at another online store. My Discover card was putting in some serious overtime.

All-in-all, I spent on necessities roughly three times the very reasonable cost of the horse. Someone wise once said "there's no such thing as a free horse", or something to that effect. Truer words were never misquoted!

To say that having a miniature horse around is a completely different experience for a die-hard big-horse owner is only partly accurate. In reality, these tiny equines have the same generous nature and immense spirit as their bigger cousins. Aside from having to seriously scale down the stall accommodations, few changes were required. Miniature horses cannot reach buckets hung at big-horse height. Within minutes of being stalled, Duke threw the mother of all tantrums, flinging his feed bucket, which was attached by a strap to the feed door for his dining convenience. The bucket landed upside-down on his head, the handle under his chin, and there he stood until I stopped laughing long enough to take it off. Buckets with handles are a problem. Feed pans are better. Rubber feed pans are best as they're heavier and harder to toss, and a manger with hay rack proved the ideal solution.

Minis are adept jumpers, so it's not necessary to replace your step-up four-horse trailer, but if it's a slant load or doesn't have a center divider that reaches the floor, you're going to have to improvise. Duke did fine in the forward section of my four-horse stock trailer once he figured out how to get in. The hay net hung low enough for him to reach kept him happily occupied until we got home. A fancy trailer with hay and feed mangers would have been a problem as he would have spent the trip standing underneath one.

Should you get a miniature horse? Sure. If you're willing to make the necessary adjustments, by all means treat yourself to a little horse. Though my experience with minis is limited, I have yet to meet one I didn't like. Don't buy a mini as a gift for a child unless you intend to oversee play time carefully. The temptation for a child to climb aboard will be strong, and a mini can be permanently injured by riding. Duke weighs about 200 pounds. Given the twenty-percent rule—a horse is capable of safely carrying twenty percent of its body weight—that would mean he could carry forty pounds. That's forty pound including saddle, pad, and clothing for the child. A child who is light enough to ride a mini probably can't sit up on his own.

On the other hand, if you're a willing teacher and overseer, I can imagine nothing more wonderful for a child than a bond with an equine small enough to be manageable. Miniature horses weren't singled out for seeing-eye and companion work just because they're cute. They tend towards patience and compassion, both great qualities for a child's pet. Just remember, it's still a horse and is fine living outside. There are no mini horse beds in the pet catalogs. I know. I checked.

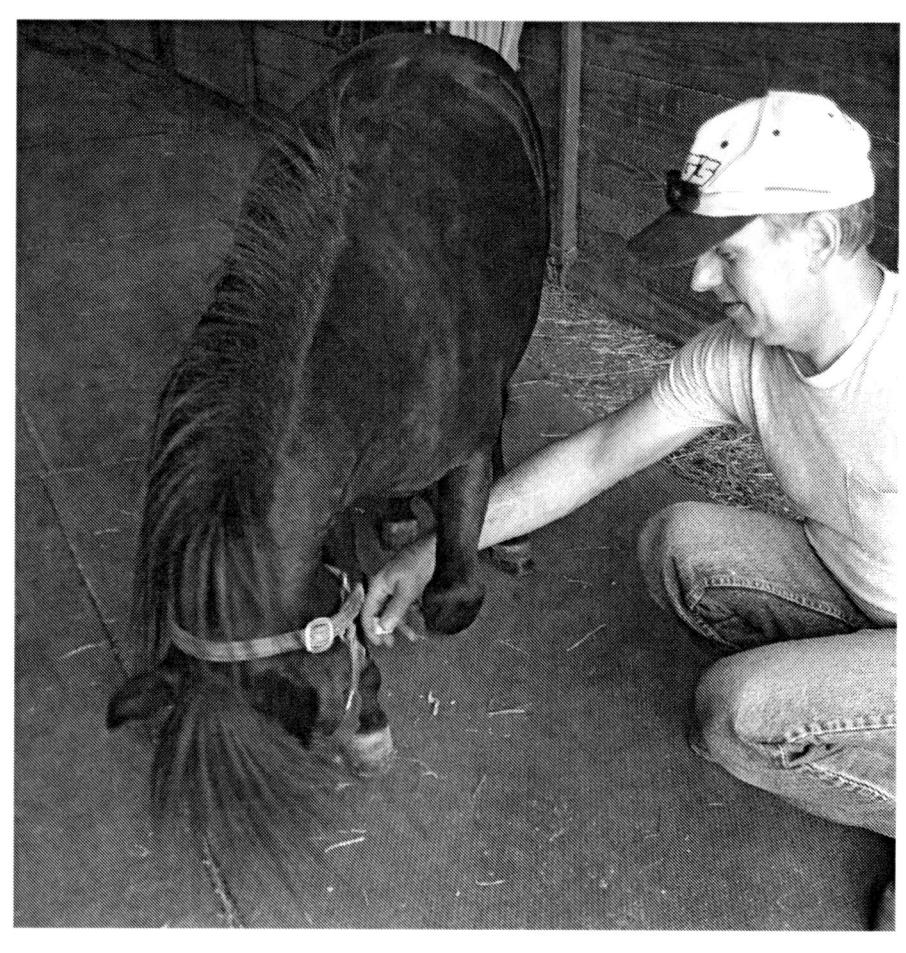

... a completely different experience.

Scaling down accommodations.

Chapter 12

My Horse Hates Me!

Kathleen was picking bits of crud out of the bloody abrasions on her arms. Her horse, Weasel, was munching happily on a pile of hay he'd dragged out of the hay stall; the looks on their faces spoke volumes. "Kathleen," I asked in amazement, "what possessed you to take him out bareback with only a halter and lead on him? He's barely broke!"

"No horse of mine needs a saddle" she shrieked, spitting dust. "If I can't take him out naked, then he's not worth keeping."

"So, what happened?"

"We got into the tall grass; something touched his butt, and the next thing I knew he was bucking across the road! Idiot! Look at this ... I'm missing half my elbow! He *hates* me, and the feeling is mutual." She turned a withering glare on her equine buddy, who gazed back at her with no expression at all.

Weasel was three and had about a month's training on him. Since birth, his attitude had echoed his dam's. Mommy Whack-a-Doodle had qualified for the Witchy Mare of the Year Pro Dingbat Finals four times. In her day, she could ignite a spark of fear in everyone who knew her. Kathleen glanced at her in the pasture where she stood—ears pinned at nothing in particular—and lamented, "His mother has always hated me, and now

Weasel is as useless as she is." Grabbing the errant gelding by the halter, she dragged him to a small paddock, locking the gate behind her, muttering under her breath something that sounded like "Alpo".

Weasel would stand in that paddock alone and wondering until Kath had lost her pique and forgiven him his transgression, giving me plenty of time to observe and assess the efficacy of the punishment. Did solitary confinement fit the crime? Had a crime, in fact, been committed, and who was the criminal? When he came out of the paddock, was he contrite and ready to do her bidding? Ha!

If there's one statement I've learned to despise over my forty-three years of horse life, it's "He *should* be able to _____ by now." Fill in the blank any way you like. Some of the most common:

- Walk without tripping
- Trot a straight line
- Canter a round circle
- Move in a frame
- Win at barrels
- Stand still for tacking-up
- Stand ground-tied while I use the bathroom at a show
- Get on the trailer without a fuss
- Jump something new without getting hysterical
- Ignore my ringing cell phone

Might as well add "drive the truck to the feed store" and "braid his own mane" for all the sense that statement makes.

Horses are better than we are in a lot of ways. They're more honest and easier to get along with. They do make bigger messes than most teenagers, and they will never learn to clean their own rooms, but they put up with our human nonsense, which earns them an extra few points. Their eyes bore into us, searching, it would seem, for a glimmer of intelligence that might give them hope. Why is it that we can't be as understanding as they are?

They expect us to learn their language since they can't speak ours, and many of us are pretty poor communicators in any forum, human or otherwise. You want a horse that walks straight, trots smoothly, canters round and in a frame (or at least comfortably and without bucking) and succeeds at whatever job you've assigned to him, and you want him to do all of it through an intuitive understanding of your goals and desires. How nuts is that? Your horse hates you? Well ... uh ...

Most horses are willing to try for a very long time to understand and comply before they develop a real hatred for their human companions. Kathleen's horse doesn't hate her; he's confused by her. She owns many horses, and has complaints about them all. She expects all of them to perform for her, but has never made any attempt to teach them what it is she wants. Not all of us are as severely impaired, but every horse owner has definite Kathleen potential. We also all have the ability to learn to teach.

More importantly, we have to be good students. We need to pay attention to the job we've taken on. If your horse isn't walking smoothly forward, if he's side-tracking, wandering, tripping over his feet, or doing a fine impression of a tourist from a foreign land, what are you doing to encourage that? Are you focused on the job at hand, or are you planning where to put the year-end trophy saddle? Do accept your young (or retraining) horse's freely-swinging, relaxed walk as a compliment to your horsemanship skills, or are you daydreaming about the ribbons you'll be winning if only your horse will shape up before the next show?

Let's talk task analysis. In simple terms, task analysis is the process of breaking down an end result into the steps required for its successful attainment. It's an important skill for everyone to learn, but even more so for horse people. If you want the living room carpet clean, you need to first get the vacuum out of the closet, blow the dust off of it, and see if you can remember where you stored the bags. If you want your horse to walk forward calmly, you have to first teach him to walk carrying your weight. Whether the issue is that he's so green he hasn't yet learned the balance required, or whether it's that he's off the track and as jiggy as a high school freshman at a senior prom, a calm, balanced walk is still a project for both of you. If you want your green-broke four-year-old to canter in a balanced frame, you need to figure out just where the process has broken down. Can he walk? Can he trot? Can you collect and extend, round and elongate at those gaits? Does he have any clue that you're talking to him at all? If you have answered any of these questions with a negative, it's time for you to go back to kindergarten and start over, whether your horse is three or thirty.

Getting past the idea that a horse of a particular age *should* be doing X, Y or Z isn't easy. We treat our horses like we treat our children: we load them up with expectations, then we withhold the tools they need to fulfill them. The kids go off and do drugs and get pregnant, and we blame anyone who can't get out of the way fast enough. The horses buck us off and become hard to catch in the field, and we curse our bad luck at having wound up with such an incorrigible beast. They're all yelling at us, and we're not listening.

Black Stallion dreams make us our own—and our horses'—worst enemies. Odds are against any prospective horse owner lucking into a "made" horse for $500. He's not going to come wandering into your front yard with a "Please Feed This Horse" tag on his halter. You're not going to walk into your local hack stable's sale barn and be handed the keys to the Perfect Horse. Spend $60,000 on a horse, and you're still going to have to learn the whys and wherefores of his operating system. He might be just as difficult and uncooperative in a matter of months as any mustang in the BLM pens if you take a lackadaisical approach to this assignment.

Famous trainers and clinicians are making a fortune thanks to our desire to see our horses reach our goals for them. The entire huge and profitable horse business hinges on our dreams. All of it is wasted on horsemen who continue believe that shortcuts exist and that they can skip to the last page of the book without hurting, confusing and, yes, incurring the wrath of their equine companions.

A nice lady I once knew got a colt in trade for an older horse she'd owned. She was very excited, but not very knowledgeable. I don't think there was a mistake she didn't make in trying to break and train that little guy. She meant well, was kind-hearted and loved him dearly, but she was anxious and ill-equipped to see the project through to a successful conclusion. She took advice from wherever it came without adding any independent thought.

In time the frightened but equally kind-hearted colt did come around, but not before he'd broken her pelvis the first time she tried to mount him. They both healed, and she took to leading him around instead of riding him. She had to stop even that when he freaked while she was hand-walking him on the trail, and he got caught in a wire fence, cutting himself almost beyond repair. Again they both survived, but she became so frightened of this hateful, scary horse that she got rid of him as soon as she could. Whether or not she got another horse, I can't say. She left the barn, and I never saw her again. Whether or not the disaster was preventable was obvious to everyone around her. It might have taken years for her and her horse to learn, side-by-side, the steps to success. Like many people who don't have their horses at home and have to pay board, she didn't want to wait that long. The green horse/green rider adage is never as true as when the green rider takes on the job of training the green horse without outside help.

Your horse doesn't hate you; he only hates that he can't understand what you want. He is truculent and as difficult as a human toddler because you have taught him to expect your inconsistency. He is tired and frustrated with the unearned punishments. He would like you a lot more if you would make some effort to really work *with* him, not just work near him. So stop your fussing and head-tossing and set your mind to the job you've taken on. You might be amazed at the change in your horse's attitude, and you'll be able to take full credit for it at the next year-end award ceremony.

Uh-oh! The price of corn is up again. Can I have the comics?

Chapter 13

▼

And Then There Was ... Synchronicity!

"Hello?"

"*Ms. Friedman? This is Jim Stanley with the Internal Revenue Service...*"

"Well, I'll be darned! You know, Jim, it seems like every time I get ready to cheat on my taxes, the phone rings, and it's you! What a coincidence!"

"*Whatever.*"

✳   ✳   ✳   ✳

Everyone's been through it. You're driving into town to pick up a quart of milk, and the thought crosses your mind that you haven't seen your aunt Lucille in months. The next thing you know, you find yourself in a series of bizarre incidents culminating with Aunt Lucille having just gotten a job behind the counter of the out-of-the-way shop in front of which your car broke down.

Coincidence? Some say not. There is a school of thought devoted to the concept that nothing is a coincidence. You only thought you didn't know

Aunt Lucille had taken up selling hairnets. Actually, your neighbor had mentioned the fact in passing and almost out of earshot. Your brain grabbed the nugget and stashed it away like the demented squirrel that it is, pulling it out of hiding just as you heard the clunking sound that presaged your car's demise. Your brain made you go there. The fact that your car was on its last legs was in no way related to Aunt Lucille.

The theory is called "Synchronicity". If you take the word apart you find "syn", which means "the same" and "chronic", which means "over time". The "ity" part is up for grabs. Synchronous events happen at the same time, but are not related to each other except for that fact.

In short, "synchronicity" theory supposes that nothing happens by accident and that it's very easy to mistake the cause of the event you're experiencing. If you were thinking of riding Lothario this afternoon, and he happened to be standing by the gate when you got to the barn, you might see a causative connection between your thoughts and Lothario's behavior. That it was near dinner time, and Lothario always stands by the gate between three P.M. and five P.M. so he won't lose his place in line, is the key, but your belief system would challenge that. You thought it; he did it, and could the Hand of the Universe be more obvious?

Naturally there's more to the theory than that—after all, someone wrote a whole book on the subject—but I won't belabor the facts here. Why spoil my record and bring facts into it at all? This was going somewhere, and before I forget the destination, I'll move on. The point is that, given a chance and a little motivation, people can believe some very odd things. In psychology this is called "superstitious behavior". In sociology it's called "religion". In technology it's called "Microsoft has shipped a new OS, and it's error free!"

Now, I hear what you're thinking. There you sit, covered with sweat (yours) and manure (not yours), and you're wondering of what possible use this information could be in the sphere of reality that is your horse-filled life.

The horse world survives on synchronicity. Without it, no one with any sense would buy a horse, own a horse, keep a horse—and certainly riding one would be out of the question. As long as we can keep the faith, keep believing that there are unseen connections between our desires and our horse's behavior—between the brand of blanket we buy and our horse's ability to perform a piaffe; between the wearing of our "lucky" breeches and the outcome of the Jack Benny Classic English Pleasure Stakes class—we will keep on plugging away.

Am I saying that all horse people live in a state of neurotic euphoria? Of course not. I, for one, can see plainly the handwriting on the barn wall. I know that no matter how hard I concentrate, Pokey is not going to jump four-foot spreads. I admit that, all my wishing and hoping aside, my fond dream of owning a first-class Western Pleasure prospect is not going to be realized until I buy a horse bred for that purpose and learn to ride better.

What is Horsedom's favorite synchronicity story? That would be the one that says you will ride into the sunset on a perfect animal if only you will take out a second mortgage on your house, sell the kids into slavery, and hand over the keys to your safe deposit box to the breeder with the biggest breed-journal ad. Have you ever been to a true horse trader's barn? The horses' values in those places are directly related to the liquidity of the prospective buyer's cash flow. The horse I turned down for two thousand dollars, for example, went ten minutes later to a Good Home for five thousand. From this experience I learned that people who adhere to synchronicity theory are also prime for investment counseling.

Where else does synchronicity theory rear its intriguing head? Think about it, and I'm sure you'll begin to see it for yourself. You rode Lothario around the far corner of the ring, and he spooked. Maybe it was a squirrel or a leaf, or it might have been the ubiquitous horse-eating mountain lion. Only Lothario knows. So what will happen the next time you round that corner? If he's a synchronisicist (say that three times fast!), he'll spook again … and again. When on the fiftieth spook, in growing depression and frustration, you drop your inside shoulder and begin humming "Bess, You Is My Woman Now", what ho! Lothario rounds the corner with no problem at all.

What happened there? Well, Lothario believed that rounding the corner caused the evil squirrel to threaten him. He also believed that spooking away from the corner made it all better. Believing that, then, he continued in that superstitious behavior until something else caught his attention and he, quite literally, forgot. And what did you do? You applied a little of your own belief system. You chose to believe that the dropping of your shoulder and the choice of tune were direct causes of Lothario's sudden decision to move around the corner without spooking. As a result, you may well continue to hum and lean for another few turns around that end of the ring till either you fall off the horse, get tired of the song, or your trainer yells, "Get that shoulder up!" Taken another step further, relying on experience to convince you that your trainer will once again become apoplectic and threaten to send you and Lothario packing if you don't obey, you straighten up and stop humming. *Voilà!* Synchronicity Theory in action.

Now, I'm not about to pass judgment on the validity or usefulness of anyone's belief system. If you share with your horse a proclivity towards superstitious thought processes, more power to you. It's a bonding thing. If you are willing to suspend disbelief long enough to think that your huffing "I think I can; I think I can" under your breath as you head through the in-gate will take you over that deadly oxer near the wall, or that if you wear your lucky underwear, Lothario won't turn his *passage* into airs above the ground again, who am I to criticize? Whatever works is fine with me. Approach any situation with confidence from whatever source, and you may well change the outcome by sheer force of will. I suggest only that you be aware that you have entered the Twilight Zone so you won't be blind-sided by reality. Look the situation square in the eye, see it for what it is, then turn quickly three times to the left and spit over your right knee before the moon rises and your next foal will be a beautiful filly destined for greatness. Trust me. I read the book.

Chapter 14

Psych!

Just like a lot of other horse owners (not to mention parents of errant teenagers), I prefer not to let on that I notice my horses' idiosyncrasies. When PMS strikes my mare, I make sure she has lots of turnout with the gelding of her choice and carrots three times a day. I carefully avoid crossing behind her when she's sporting that steady, "Just try me!" glare. When my sensitive Quarter Horse, Leos Languishing Spirit, slips under his stall guard and spends the night piling blankets and manure in front of said PMS-ing mare's stall, I may get a tad grumpy, but I try not to let it show as I drag him back to his assigned space. I can ignore the wise-guy Morgan's sneaking into a vacant stall to check for uneaten grain, and the one-eyed Appy can spend the rest of his life in his stall if that's what he wants to do. In general, I'm a pretty laid-back, take-it-with-a-grain-of-salt kind of horse owner.

I take exception, however, to being put in imminent, startling, ER-quality personal danger. Zipperdoodle crossed the line when he used a squirrel in the shrubbery as an excuse for a wild-eyed, rearing shy across the lawn. He crossed the lawn alone, as I was engaged in counting my teeth and feeling for broken bones at the time. I knew this was the end of the line because he came back for me. No truly paranoid horse would come back for his rider, right?

As luck would have it, just about then an article appeared in one of the dozen or so horse magazines that fill my mailbox. It was as if the author had read my mind! The key to sorting out my scary situation lay in the fact that my big baby of a gelding had never been properly started. He'd been Lyons-ed and Centered and had his psyche probed, but somehow I'd allowed a gap in his learning process akin to skipping a toddler's potty-training lessons. As a result of my lapse, a control issue had arisen. Trust me; you don't want to battle for control with a critter that dwarfs your car.

So it happened that I launched a full-frontal assault on my gelding's missing spook training. The magazine article suggested the use of a mattress, not as a soft spot for a foolhardy owner to land when de-spooking goes awry, but as a threatening object to be bravely mastered. The article's author knows whereof he speaks. Sgt. Rick Pelicano, author of *Bomb-Proof Your Horse,* is a mounted police officer who trains horses to be safe and sane in the worst of circumstances. I defy any horse owner to deny dreaming of owning one of those amazing police horses who stride into a rowdy crowd with eyes level and not a spook in sight. We'd all have to be nuts to take the hard line and shout, "Hey! Give me a mare who bucks at the sight of air and a gelding who's terrified of leaves, and I'll be a happy camper. No bomb-proof horses for me!" Sorry, but that's just plain silly. Maybe I'm getting old, but living through a trail ride has become a meaningful goal.

The article called for a mattress, which the equine would first inspect, then, predictably, jump over, and finally walk across. This exercise would result in a horse who could 1) face the unexpected with flair and élan, and 2) be welcome in any Holiday Inn in the country. With winter just ending, and the results of a three-month layoff yet to be felt, I was looking forward to grabbing my clicker, my mattress, and a bag of frosted mini-wheats and heading for the round pen. Unfortunately, I was thwarted by the sheer weight of the mattress. I was more than willing to donate my guest room bedding to the cause, but dragging it out to the barn proved more than I could handle.

I spent some quality time in the garage and storage sheds before finally scaring up a suitable bogey. The brightly-colored floor pillow was hardly as threatening as a mattress, but far easier to carry, and given Zip's flightiness, I figured it was a good place to start. Armed with my bright red and orange flea market boogeyman, I headed for the barn. Even my incredibly brave (read: "too young to understand long-term disability") daughter was surprised that I was tacking up the monster boy for the first ride of the season. I'm not stupid, only seriously impaired, so I did grab the longe line and give him a few minutes to work the kinks out before I hopped aboard. All indications to the contrary, he was fine. I rode him through a dressage test, around some barrels, and over a few cross-rails before heading for the pen and our round of pillow training.

Truthfully, the rest of the experience was a disappointment. I was ready for whatever Zip would throw at me. I did some deep breathing and shook out my tight muscles like a fighter entering the ring. Before showing Zip the pillow, I worked him, Lyons-style, for a minute.

When the moment of truth arrived, Zip, as always, surprised the heck out of me. I threw the pillow on the ground and ducked, waiting for the explosion. There was nothing. In fact, he didn't seem to see it. I picked it up and showed it to him, then dropped it at his feet. He walked around it and resumed his "turn-and-face" position. I tried to get him to step on it, but he politely stepped over it. I waved it in the air, threw it on the ground, and, finally, tossed it towards him, all with no response from the Zip-boy.

Just when I thought the entire session had been a waste of time, the light-bulb went on over Zip's head. I saw it and urged him on, "C'mon Zip! Step on it! Here! Put your foot here!" He smiled, lifted his front hoof and planted it firmly in the middle of the pillow. The crowd went wild! He smiled wider, ducked his head, grabbed the pillow in his teeth, and, using his hoof to hold it down, pulled a large chunk out of the center. This trophy he presented to me with a flourish, a reflection of the passing grade he earned in Clicker Training 101: Retrieving Stuff for Mommy.

That was it. Our spook training will have to resume when I've worked up the energy to drag something larger and more threatening outside. Meanwhile, I continue to scour the catalogs for a remedy for Rustleophobia ("fear of squirrels") and keep a good thought for the day when a trail ride won't require a reservation at the ER "just in case".

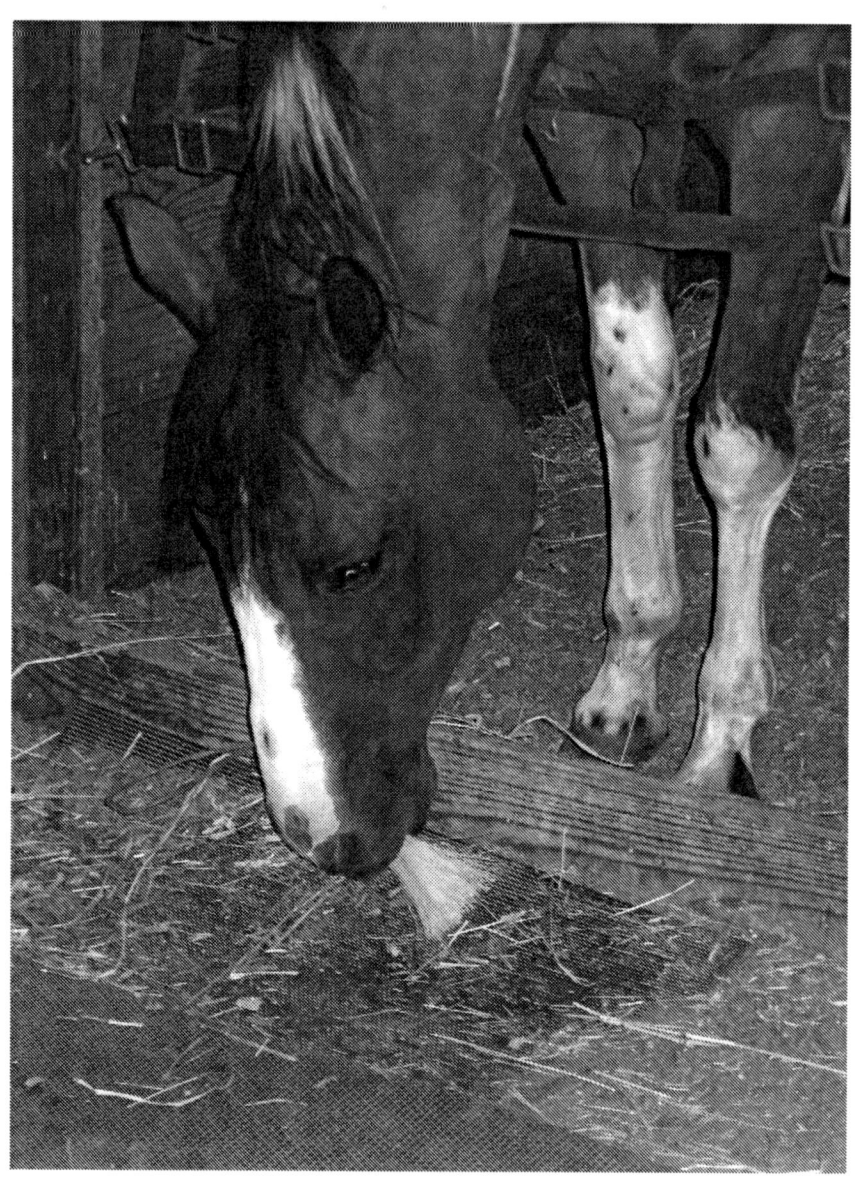

*Topping the Learning Curve
Don't hire barn help; train it!*

Chapter 15

That's "Latent", Not "Lazy" Learning

My big Paint gelding, Zipsonmyfootagain, is very fussy about his girth. More than fussy, he's downright psychotic about it. If there's so much as one hair rubbed the wrong way under that strap, he will shimmy and shake, kick out and twitch until he settles it, even if that means that I wind up watching from a seat on the ground. This is his one, huge quirk that we've never managed to overcome. Every ride is prefaced by a lengthy tacking-up process involving considerable brushing and stretching his legs to release any tiny smidge of crinkled skin that might be pinched under the most expensive, softest, ergonomically-shaped girth available on this planet. That's still not enough for him, but more than enough work for me.

I've considered the possibility that some of his gyrations might fall into the Creative Malingering category, but since discussion with a dancing behemoth tends to be unsuccessful, I opted to at least take the burden of correction off myself and put it where it belongs. If he's got a problem he's going to have to step up and solve it. To this end, armed with my trusty clicker and a bag of carrot chunks, I launched an educational program geared to teaching him to do his own adjusting *before* we get into the ring for our Level Onlykidding dressage test.

It should have been simple to get him to stretch his front legs either on command or by cue, and eventually on girthing and again before mounting. Task analysis is key, and I am an ace at analyzing tasks. We already had the "pick-it-up" cue down perfectly so the farrier or prospective hoof-picker needed only to point at the selected foot and say "pick it up". Not very exciting as cues go, but unmistakable. He was running about 80% accuracy on that one. Getting him to lift the same foot forward and stretch was, in my opinion, a simple case of building on the existing behavior. Follow the "pick-it-up" by pulling the leg forward until the auto-stretch mechanism kicks in, and click-treat. I followed all the rules, making sure to stand in a different location for each of the two desired behaviors, look him in the eye to make sure he noticed the difference, and stifle my moans and groans as he fought me for control of his leg so he wouldn't think those were part of the cue.

That part was actually rather successful. A few sessions with the massage therapist and I was standing upright again and breathing normally.

The next part—the "add a verbal cue" part—followed right along. I thought "stretch" seemed appropriate. It sounded very much unlike "pick-it-up", so confusion would not be an issue. At the same time, in an effort to kill two birds, I included a tap on the shoulder with the tickler on my dressage whip. Killing two birds with one stone is probably a whole lot easier as birds generally don't have a sense of humor.

Ignoring the antics that accompanied his learning curve, ducking the well-placed "stretch" when my back was turned and my butt fair game, keeping a clicker attached to my wrist at all times and my pockets slimy with carrot crud, I took every "teachable moment" and turned it into the highlight of our training session. Still, when the snow began to make reading seem more attractive than riding, he still wasn't giving me his all. As with so many other behaviors I'd tried—and failed—to instill in him (*not* holding the bridle in his mouth while I was trying to put it on was a big zero on my scoreboard), this project seemed hopeless.

With the ground finally iced over completely, I gave up the game. I'd start again in the spring when I was more enthusiastic and he was feeling less Larry the Cable Guy.

Then came the rare December day when the temperature spiked from sub-zero to a balmy 44 degrees. The ice retreated, and off to the barn I went in my winter-fat fleece pull-ons and my big puffy boots. Zip seemed delighted at the prospect of a ride. I wouldn't have used "delighted" to describe the giraffe-on-crack Tigger bounce down the barn aisle, but the gleam in his eye belied his joy. I dragged the forty-pound blanket off his back, gave him a quick, high-static brushing, and threw the pad and saddle on. I hadn't even taken the girth off its special girth hook when he stretched with his left front foot. Huh! A pat and a carrot chunk seemed in order. He thought so too as the minute I grabbed the girth, he stretched his right foot.

I have degrees in psychology and education. Latent learning isn't new to me. It's been an accepted explanation and part of the Natural Horsemanship training phenomenon for years. In some circles it's called "let 'im think about it". In others, "move on and come back; it'll sink in". In mine, "God *damn* this horse is stubborn! I need a cup of tea."

Regardless of approach and labeling, the process is an intriguing one. If a thinking entity is presented with something new that they are expected to learn but don't quite "get" the first four thousand times, they will continue to replay the mental tape of the episode at odd moments. Then one day something will pop, and learning will appear. Zip and I had one of those popping moments.

You can put this bit of learning theory to work for you, or you can let it work against you. If you use to it your advantage, you will repeat a stimulus/response pairing (that's Psychologese for "cue-click-treat till your brain numbs out") until you see just the beginnings of learning taking place. Then, against your better judgment, you'll quit for a bit and go on to something else—something he already knows or that is somehow connected to the task at hand—and let the new process rumble around in his brain for a bit. It'll be bumped and sloshed by other stuff he's trying to learn, like how to open the feed room door and partake of the all-you-can-eat buffet. It will attach itself to other behaviors and synchronously to whatever was going on around him while you were trying to get him to focus. It will detach and form new alliances. It will dance the kazatsky. You'll go home and watch the first three John Lyons tapes again.

Then one day, when you're trying to teach him something entirely different (or wrestling the bridle brow band out of his teeth), he'll perform. He'll stare you right in the eye and sing "Too Sexy For My Shirt", or whatever it was you thought he'd never learn. You'll dance and laugh and give him the last of the holiday sugar cookies, and a fine time will be had by all … and this is where the "working against you" part comes in.

While he was latent learning, he was also cogitating on the best way to use his new skill. Zip demonstrated for me. When we finally finished tacking up—a feat which took a bit longer than usual as he needed to stretch each leg forty-leben times—we headed to the ring. We got halfway through the gate and needed to stretch again. Then we did the traditional FOD (foreign object debris) walk-down of the de-iced path we'd be riding on, and stretched six more times. At the mounting block, each time I put my foot in the stirrup, another urge to stretch just came over him like a rapture.

The first eighteen stretches earned him carrots and kudos. When the sun began to set on our morning ride and he was still stretching at the mounting block, I had my own "ah-hah" moment, told him enough was enough, waited for the disappointed sigh, and climbed aboard.

I will say that it was a most pleasant ride. Not once did he feel the need to wriggle like an old lady settling her girdle. He didn't kick out to the side to release that single hair going the wrong direction under the girth. He didn't look back at me in apology as I remounted for the third time. We just rode. As we did, I discovered that he had latently learned the headset we'd worked on and the whole "stop" thing, which had not been his forte. Yee-hah!

There is wisdom in the old saw, "Just give him time". There's also wisdom in keeping yourself flexible and knowing in your heart that this whole horse thing is a dance, not a science. If you get one step that you asked for, you've done something special. Go have that cup of tea and revel in the fact that you've been given a moment to remember while you still have the mental capacity to remember it.

Why lessons? Any other questions?

Chapter 16

In Defense of the Pros

Backyard horse owners know a secret. It's this: we can be good as our word at any riding discipline as long as no one is watching. Ask me if my horse can jump, and I'll tell you no lies. Sure he can. All of my horses can jump. They can run barrels and poles, rope, pen, fox hunt and do dressage. Now ask me if I can do those things.

Hedging comes naturally to horse people. We sell horses that are "serviceably sound" (on the three remaining legs) and buy horses that have "no vices" (except for that cribbing thing). We take Grand at "unrated" (read: "backyard fun day") shows and display our ribbons proudly. Backyard horse people are a breed unto themselves, and I am their queen.

But even the most resistant of us eventually comes a-cropper of a tide-turner. It can be a horse not reaching it's full potential (like that filly in the side paddock that still has a chunk of your pj's in her teeth from this morning's grooming session), or the lust that comes on all of us after the Olympics or National Pro Finals Rodeo. Whatever the reason, we all eventually harbor the thought that maybe … perhaps … just possibly … we need a few lessons.

My announcement that I've recently begun taking dressage lessons from a local luminary garnered mixed reactions. The most common question was, "Why?" Not "why him?", but, more pointedly, "why lessons?" The answer should have been obvious. No one comes home from work, throws a horse on a trailer and hauls it away to sweat for an intense hour without some sort of sincere need to do so. No one works as hard as I work *in* that lesson without a serious desire to accomplish something that cannot be accomplished otherwise. Certainly no one pays cash money for the privilege without some soul-searching.

I searched my soul at great length before defecting into the lesson program. This has been a stop-and-start thing, but at last my aging, claustrophobic Quarter Horse, Leo, my trainer, and I have settled into a routine of sorts. Leo still shakes and sweats on the trailer. My trainer is patient but forceful. I am obsessed. Together, we are a beautiful thing.

Like a woman saved from the desert, I am horribly, intensely, irreparably thirsty for knowledge. Bless me, Lester, for I have sinned. It has been (… what? Fifteen years?) a very long time since my last *real* riding lesson.

I'm sure my trainer has better students, but none so sincere. My sincerity has redoubled since my daughter (bless her pointed little head) videotaped my last lesson. Have I really been riding for a century with one foot stuck out and my shoulders down around my waist? Is "kick-'im-and-pray" truly not an acceptable canter cue? Have I been fooling myself into believing that it was the horse who wouldn't bend, when, in fact, it was me, stiff as a board on the side where my briefcase and purse normally hang? And when did my boobs move into my armpits? *There's* a shirt I'll never wear in public again!

I've already learned a lot in the few weeks since I entered this new stage in my riding life. I've learned how to sit. I've learned not to talk back. I've learned that a really nice circle is almost as good as sex. I've learned that horses are smart and forgiving. I've learned that learning is key to everything in this life.

Yesterday I lucked into a Curt Pate clinic at a Quarter Horse show. While he painlessly guided a young mare into her first saddle-up, he told us that his whole approach to training and horsemanship has changed in the past two years. He said that he'd seen some things and learned some things and realized that even a long-time pro (he was one of the two trainer-consultants on the *Horse Whisperer* movie) can sometimes have an awakening, an "A-ha!" moment when he realizes that everything he thought he knew was wrong.

He told us that there's nothing natural about natural horsemanship when the goal is a horse with his head on backwards running sideways and all bunched up with stress. He also told us that whatever we are trying to do with our horses we need to give them and ourselves time. "In your own time" was the way he phrased his training schedule. And he told us that the more we torture our horses—forcing them into "frames", putting "head-sets" on them, making them spin and slide and all that other stuff that no horse ever thought of on his own—the more time off we need to give them to balance it out.

The ninety-or-so minutes that I spent in the scorching sun, slack-jawed and wide-eyed while the Master's voice washed all my set-in-stone ideas away did nothing so much as make me realize that riding lessons aren't all on horseback, and that there's no such thing as too old, too experienced, or too good.

When the infernal heat finally lets up, I'll head back up to my trainer's, this time with Zips Bombshell in the trailer and a whole new perspective in my head. And while I'm at it, I think I'll call around and see who else is giving what kind of lessons around here. It's never too late to learn; we're only too stubborn and foolish to admit we need to know more.

CHAPTER 17

REAL HORSE TV!

"Reality" television shows have become as common as manure and almost as much fun. Who would have guessed that *Survivor* would spawn an entire generation of programming that amounts to little more than mindless rubbernecking and almost-invisible marketing ploys? Everything has become Extreme, from sports to animals to food-ingestion practices (who can forget the monkey-brain incident?), and from makeovers, personal and home, to weddings and relationships. We've watched a few strangers choose their spouses from groups of hand-picked candidates and others sit vapidly by while the public votes them a life partner. What raucous fraternity-party brain trust comes up with this stuff? We've seen folks lied to and tricked, photographed secretly and exposed before millions of viewers for the idiots that they are. What's next? *Extreme Double Secret Home and Spouse Emergency Makeover and Surgery Festival?* Sign me up!

The title of Most Questionable TV Series is still up for grabs, but I'm going to put in a quick pitch for the makeover shows. I stopped watching *What Not to Wear* when I recognized my favorite Hawaiian shirt hanging on the no-no rack, and the "Fab Five" (*Queer Eye for the Straight Guy*) were unable to interest me in the ugly-duckling-to-swan guys they rebuilt from spare parts. *Extreme Makeover*, however, is a train wreck I just can't take my eyes off of. I have long been a proponent of the "It's Mine; I'll Learn to Love It" self-esteem philosophy, so when I found myself scanning the phone book for dentists who use the "Zoom" whitening method and doctors capable of un-spidering my leg veins, I had to take a step back.

If you've ever shown horses, you already suffer from self-image issues, and you've been living a reality show for however long you've been a horse person. Western pleasure riders, those glittery slinkies were never intended for anyone over the age of 14 or with significant boobage in need of restriction. English riders, the folks at Tailored Sportsman must have legs like a piano bench, or they wouldn't design pants with a seam below the knee right where last night's cannoli have gone to nest. Look at the photos that accompany most horse magazine articles, and you sure aren't going to see my thighs eclipsing the flaps on a sexy Pessoa saddle. You're going to see the "after" pictures from an extreme equestrian makeover.

So, when are we going to see a show on the Horse Network just for us? The *What Not to Wear* crew have yet to address the issues that plague the horsy. I've seen many a fashion emergency at the farms where I've boarded. In many cases, it was me! Why is no one worried about me? What am I, chopped liver?

I would like to propose a Horse Reality Show. I'm thinking a twelve-week season, broken into three parts.

Part One: Extreme Bodywork

The first four weeks of the season would focus on dragging unwilling horse folks from their barns and chaining them up in various salons, hospitals and gyms. Day after day they would be sliced, diced, firmed, toned and rearranged until each of them—men and women alike—looked like that girl in the ads for the new low-rise schooling breeches.

Part Two: Extreme Togs

Once the body work is complete, each subject in this sociological experiment would be given a new wardrobe of riding clothes appropriate to his or her discipline of choice. The togs will be pricy, dry-clean-only, and so stylish they have not yet appeared in even the best catalogs. There will be genuine diamonds on the designer slinkies, real shadbellies in the dressage coats, and eventers will have color-coordinated body armor, custom-fitted and autographed by Lara Croft and whatever Big Name Trainer is in vogue (and in need of marketing) at that point. Product placement is everything, so expect to see subtle labels everywhere, including on the Zoom-whitened smiles.

Part Three: Extreme Horses

This is where Real Horse TV will outshine the competition. While the wusses on other reality makeover shows are having their apartments redecorated, our participants will be having their horses "done". Our own makeover staff will consist of the O'Connors, the Leone brothers, John Lyons, George Morris, and GaWaNi Ponyboy. While our participants are having their butts tucked and their hair helmet-proofed, their horses will be flown to Rancho Someplace for a complete retraining and spa treatment. Fat horses will be thinned; thin horses will be buffed out. Stodgy English pleasure horses will learn to cut cows and run barrels. Western trail horses will become eventers. Each horse will be re-engineered to complement its owner's new look and maximize its own potential as Equus Supreme.

The final episode will be a horse show. The home audience will vote for their favorite horse and rider combination, and they will have the opportunity to mix-and-match horses and owners by clicking buttons on a website. Losers will appear the following week on *Extreme Depression,* where normal horse people in jeans, T-shirts and Wal Mart leggings will come together to be secretly videotaped leafing through horse-stuff catalogs and repeating the words, "Think we'll get out of here in time for a trail ride?"

Chapter 18

The Breeding Bug

If there's a horseman reading this who has never, not once, not for a fleeting second considered breeding a horse, I'll eat my mini. Staunch supporter that I am of the total eradication of irrational, emotional breeding decisions, I would have gone to the soapbox with all the fervor of a TV Evangelist before I would have entered the backyard breeding game. Then I met Duke.

Duke, formally known as "Lazy A Blue Mist", will hereinafter be referred to as "Piglet". He's Piglet in attitude, Piglet in appearance, and Piglet in the raucous squealy-squally noises he makes seemingly without pause. I know he breathes between screams, but you can't prove it by listening.

Not only was I not interested in breeding, I also wasn't in the market for a miniature horse. I was looking for a fifteen-hand, broke-to-death, trail-and-traffic-safe Quarter Horse to keep around for those moments when family, friends and I might need amusement of that nature. The Internet had lit up my monitor with pictures of likely prospects, and I was in the process of narrowing down the location when Duke appeared.

I was tired. I'd been shopping too long. I didn't notice the "miniature" part until I'd already fallen in love with the photo. I didn't notice the "stallion" part until much later. Those are my excuses.

As so many horse deals do, this one came out of left field. Calling on the only person I know who actually knows anything about 1) miniature horses and 2) miniature stallions, I set about making the decision in the most logical way possible. Being as horse-shopping road trips are always a source of glee, we'd go together to see him, and afterwards I'd pretty much flip a two-headed coin. The decision was made when the picture popped up on my screen, not when I walked into the barnyard with my guru. The rest was just window dressing.

I did hedge my bet as best my emotional makeup would allow. I asked my friend if she would help me place the little guy if he didn't work into my herd. She agreed, and that was that. No thought of what all of this would entail impinged on my besotted brain.

Piglet's arrival on the farm is chronicled elsewhere in this book, so I'll spare you the retelling and go right to the heart (and other private parts) of the matter. Suffice it to say that I had "standing at stud" on my web site and an insane gleam in my eye before the day was out. I'd called and emailed everyone I knew who owned a pony or mini mare. I was about to be a Breeder.

A stallion is a bundle of hormones barely contained by flesh. Walk into a stud barn, and you'll be bowled over by a cloud of lust. The screams and snorts of a stallion are rooted in the Pleistocene and slam into the innocent bystander like a bus. A small stallion is a big stallion in a tiny suit. His only saving grace is that you are bigger than he is, and you can most likely knock him down when he gets too big for his britches and leaves hoof prints on your chest. Piglet's squeals are piercing and elemental and do not encourage discussion.

Here's a scenario you should consider as you work yourself up to joining the proud throng of stallion owners:

You've got a big, horny horse on the end of a flimsy piece of rope, and he's fresh off the trailer from East Somewhere. The chain across his nose may give you some sense of comfort, but it's about as useful as fly spray on a manure pile. In the pasture some fence rows away is a mixed bag of geldings and mares. If you haven't been using that gym membership, now's when you're going to regret your laziness. That primordial drive that will well up in your new guy will be more than either of you can control. He'll flip his lip in a flemen at the scent of the mare, and off he'll go. I recommend that you let go of the rope before you become parallel with the ground. The landing will hurt less.

The mare isn't exactly a slouch, either. She may be old, infirm, and as sexless (in your eyes) as your grandmother, but in that instant of recognition, she became his property, his beloved, the one he will move fences for, the one who will be the mother of his children. There is little you can do to stem the tide once it has hit the shore, so a few precautions are in order before you reach tsunami stage and are left to sort out the bumps and bruises (yours) and the broken fence boards and torn flesh (theirs) that can come with novice breedership.

Prepare before, not after the stud's arrival.

The stallion you bought was great at his last owner's farm. He behaved like a champion for grooming, shoeing, fussing, boot-application and leading to the trailer. He loaded without a hitch. If you're smart, you checked him out several times before you bought him. You're reading this book, so we can assume you're not that smart. You did, however, ask all the appropriate questions and checked the vet for bruising when he emerged from the stall after the vet check. The horse was perfect. He even stood like a statue while mares were paraded past him closely enough to exchange phone numbers. You just *know* this is going to be a great experience and a fun new project. You might even make some money at it.

That thinking is wrong on just *so* many levels! First, the stallion was at home. There's the first mistake. Visit any male in his own environment and you're likely to see him relaxed and at ease. If you can arrange to meet on neutral turf—Olive Garden comes to mind—males of any species will be more likely to show their true colors.

Second, those were familiar mares he was ignoring. He might as well have stuck a hoof in his girth and hunkered back in his stall to watch the

Bays play the Palominos in the Scooper Bowl. He knew those mares would still be around after the game, so there was no need for him to rouse himself when they blew by tittering about the latest mane styles.

Third, consider drugs. Not for yourself. Think about the idea that the stallion might just possibly have been given a little something to calm his nerves before your arrival. If you'd snuck up on him a day early, you might have seen a far different horse. I'm not suggesting that everyone with a stallion for sale is harboring a shelf full of horsy highs, but it happens, especially when it's vital that the horse be gone as soon as possible.

Don't count on the big guy being equally calm and unflappable at your place. Before you bring him home, make the necessary arrangements. Little stallions like Piglet are small enough to be contained by four-foot fences. Big stallions are not. Ask your insurance agent. Five foot fences for the stallion's enclosure are a must. If he's a jumper, you might want to go to six feet. Solid walls are good. Slip-board fencing is bad. Concrete, brick and treated oak are good. A single strand of electric is bad. If you have no place where you could safely leave a moving freight train for an hour, don't bring the stud home until you do.

Look at your herd through a stallion's eyes.

The young, the weak, and the infirm will not be able to stand up to the boldness of a stallion. I'm not saying that all stallions are wild and crazy guys, but there will come moments when he's working his way up in the herd hierarchy when death may well be imminent for your favorite old gelding. You look at that old guy and think, "safe ride". He looks at the same horse and thinks, "easy pickin's". As small as Piglet is (and believe me, anything under three feet is *tiny* by all standards), he terrorized the elder statesman of the herd until I was forced to separate them for everyone's sake. Gone was the sweet, accommodating broke-to-drive cutesy-pie mini, and in his place was a tiny demon, breathing fire and running hell-bent with his neck snaked to the ground.

The mares will all go into heat immediately. Not possible? Watch. They might all have been in season last week, but the new boy will still bring out the slut in them. They will be of no help to you in your efforts to maintain some decorum around the barn. They will call to him, whistle, shake their heads, wink, and pee copiously while you hang onto that bit of rope attached to his halter and try to explain to him that you're not ready yet.

Unless it's your plan to let the new guy breed the mares at will, you're going to need to separate them, and that doesn't just mean putting them in separate paddocks. If they can nose over the fence, you've got a disaster in the offing. Fence posts cannot stand up to the pressures of equine social interactions. Electric wire is no deterrent. I've known of a filly who attempted to get to a stallion some pastures away by jumping a five-foot fence with hot wire at the top. She was burned badly, rendered unconscious by the shock, and had to receive CPR in order to keep her alive. Guess what she did the minute she came to. She immediately began screaming for the stallion. Left alone, she would have been stuck on the same fence in minutes. Turn off the wire unless you're absolutely sure the horses are afraid enough of it to stay away. Then turn it off anyway.

You'll need to put both distance and a solid barrier between the stallion and the mares. Locking him in a stall is usually a bad idea unless you have lots of stalls you can move him to when he breaks out the walls in the first one. Even a mild-mannered gelding can take down a stall in a fit of pique. Don't let your fantasy get in the way of sane barn management. Pent-up desire is a strong force for evil.

Think twice, and act once.

As a first-time stallion owner, you are in a pickle, but it needn't be terminal. Build the enclosure you know your new guy will need, set up horsekeeping in such a way as to keep everyone safe and sound, then go to your house and pour yourself a drink. This is paper-and-pencil time. Somewhere you've got that vet book that tells you all about mares' fertility cycles and stallions' behavior. Ignore the screaming going on outside and figure out which of your mares (if any) you actually intend to breed. Note that it takes a long time for a baby horse to be born. Make sure that your timing is such that you will be equally thrilled ten months down the road when that baby hits the ground as you were when the stud's former owner handed you the keys to your new life.

If you don't intend to breed your own mares, if you've got it in your head that you will be standing your boy "at stud" for mare owners far and wide, figure out which months of the year you will be doing that. Generally, babies want to be born when the weather is fairly suitable for them to be viable. If you've got a nice, warm barn with extra big stalls where mares can safely give birth and take care of newborn horses, the weather is less of an issue. If you don't, then you probably aren't going to want to stand foal watch in a run-in in mid-blizzard. Figure out when winter is likely to end in your neck of the woods and count back eleven months. That's the earliest breeding date you should aim for.

On the other side of the coin, you don't want the baby to be born too close to winter or he might not survive anywhere but in your living room. If you live in an area where winter weather is an issue, figure out when the last day of pleasant temperatures is likely to be and count back ten months. That's your latest available date for breeding. In my area of the Northeast United States, breeding is generally limited by average backyard breeders to December (babies will be born around September and turn three months before winter arrives) through the end of May (babies will be born around March, when farm owners begin to thaw and can tolerate foal watch). If you were to advertise, you might specify those beginning and ending dates as your personal breeding season.

Of course, if they're not your mares, you needn't be so concerned. A mare being kept in a cozy barn with lots of humans around to take part in the foaling business can be bred anytime. That's up to the mare owner. You can negotiate your dates as the spirit moves you.

Which brings us to the nuts-and-bolts "how" part of this "how-to". Usually the mares come to the stallion. In all my years around horses, I've only rarely seen a stallion travel to breed mares. Generally the mare comes to the stallion's abode and stays there for three days to a month to be sure he hits the moment when she's actually fertile. For stylish brood mares, that amounts to a 30-second window once a month, while the average unpapered pasture ornament will be fertile roughly 364 days a year. Letting the stallion have his way with the mare in a specially assigned and decorated paddock is called "live cover" breeding.

If you're not into playing host to visiting females, you can consider artificial insemination. That's a whole other game, and you would need to learn all about semen collection (oh, joy!), cooling and shipment and buy the equipment to do all of that. Or you can have a vet on hand to inseminate the mare on the spot. Only you know what will work in your situation.

Always give a "live foal guarantee" (called an "LFG" among breeders). That means if the baby doesn't survive or the pregnancy doesn't go to term, you breed the mare again for free or refund the owner's money. It's the least you can do and it'll be good for business.

The Endgame

After all is said and done, you may well decide that stallion ownership is not worth the expense and work involved. Unless the stallion is an older fellow, you may still be able to have him gelded. He most likely won't be a whole lot mellower, but you'll be able to safely turn him out with the mares without accidentally committing yourself to raising a foal. Sometimes gelding does wonders to calm a stallion. It's a tough call. Work with your vet and bow to his or her expertise.

Reselling a stallion isn't easy. You did note the excited expression on the face of the former owner of your guy when you handed over the cash. Selling a horse is often difficult under the best of circumstances; that he's a stallion may double or triple the time it will take. If he's ugly, knock-kneed, buck-toothed, and frequently runs headlong into walls, you've got little chance of finding him a good home. Your folly is not likely to turn into someone else's problem.

With luck, you're reading this before you've joined the ranks of erstwhile breeders who are filling pastures with foals of questionable parentage, swelling the numbers of unwanted horses even as we watch. Think twice, do what you feel is right, and know that the Black Stallion is only fiction.

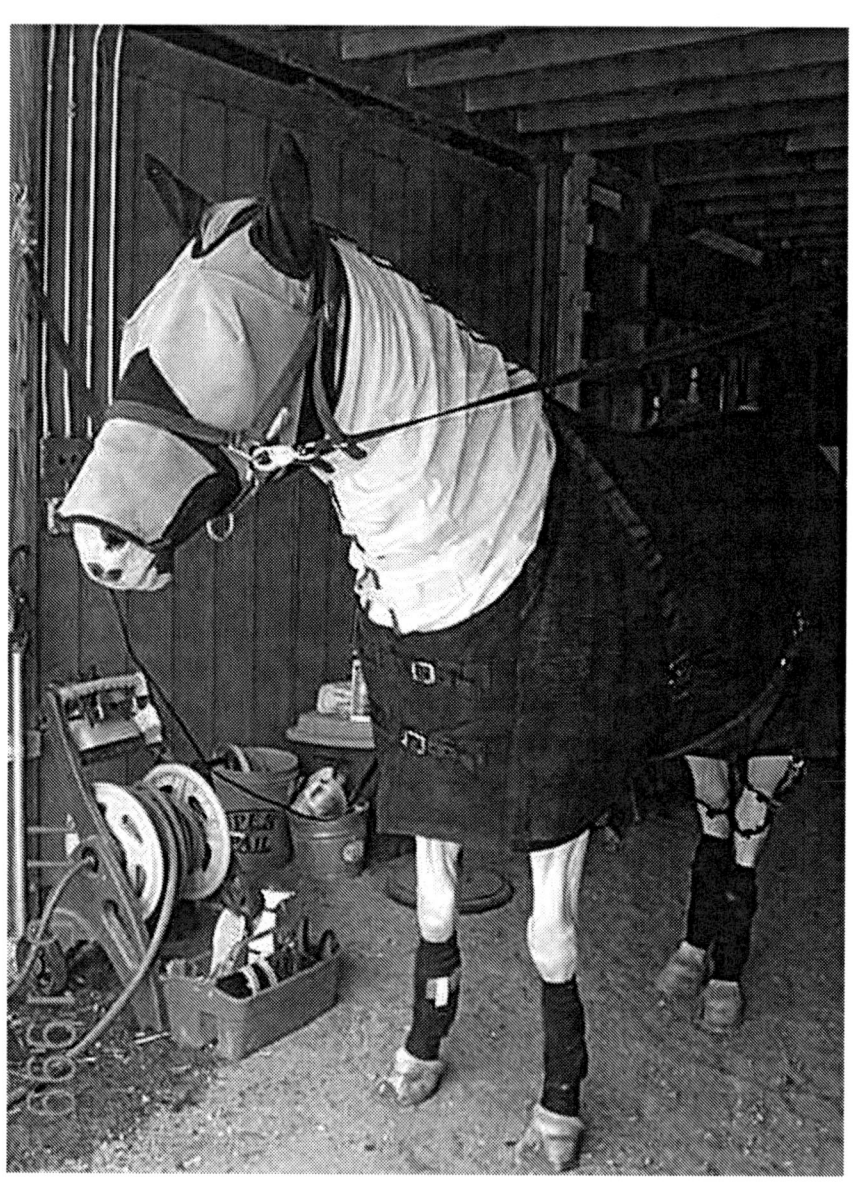

Our next model is sporting a jazzy little pre-show number ...

Chapter 19

Stuff and Nonsense

Years ago *Playboy Magazine* (who would have guessed?) ran an article on horseback riding. The details have faded from memory with the passage of time, but the gist was intriguing enough to remain. The article proclaimed riding to be the absolute best sport known to man. How so? Because, it has the best "stuff".

Most sports offer participants the option of buying high-, moderate- or low-end equipment. Generally speaking, beginners go cheap. As one becomes more accomplished, the lure of more expensive equipment begins to exert a stronger pull. The sense of accomplishment and pride that comes with no longer needing an oxygen break during a tennis game is sufficient to warrant a move up to better sneakers and day-glo balls. Among horsemen, no increase in talent, ability or accomplishment is necessary. Two weeks into horse ownership a horseman will be ready for a new saddle, a monogrammed riding jacket and a pair of Ariat mules or Tony Lama custom boots to wear around town. These are the badges that identify the bearer as part of a clique with unquestionable cachet. They are gang colors, flaunted with pride, and they cost a bundle.

If you are already hooked on riding, this is not news to you. Equine stuff manufacturers have infallible radar, and they can fill your mailbox with catalogs before the ink is dry on the transfer papers for your new horse. My first horse cost me $800, a tremendous bargain if you like older, extremely unpleasant, attitudinal mares. It never even occurred to me that I wasn't going to get far without a certain minimum number of add-ons. The sale barn had a tack shop. I was inducted into the gang with a flash of my credit card.

The horse cost me $800. The halter, bridle, saddle, pads, lead rope, brushes, brush box and bottle of horse shampoo cost me $1400. Obviously I was a beginner's beginner. I could ride, but I had not yet learned to shop. That the horse-to-stuff differential was only $600 was a dead giveaway. I've made up for it in spades in the twenty years since.

So, ready or not, if you've chosen to follow the path of the horse, you are part of an elite group whose spending power is legendary, and whose sport loyalty is beyond reproach. On any given day you can go to any tack shop in any neighborhood and find something—anything—you don't already own and *have* to have. You can upgrade your upgrades until you go to your grave. Horse stuff for riding, horse stuff for wearing when you're not riding, horse stuff to decorate your home … the assortment is endless. You can buy horse wallpaper, equestrian-themed dinnerware, toilet paper roll holders made of horse shoes, and horse-hiney mailboxes. Diamond-encrusted horse heads adorn your ears and fingers. If you can imagine it and find a place for it, someone will sell it to you. If it's something that has existed in the real world for generations, someone will put a picture of a horse on it and double the price … and you'll pay it gladly.

Horse stuff is invariably of unusually high quality. Walk into the tack room in any stable, and inhale the warm smell of fine leather. The cheapest riding boots are made of better materials than the most expensive shoes in most closets. Feel the fine wool of a hunt coat, and compare it to the rest of the items in your closet. It's likely that the rest will appear rough and ignorant by comparison. Couture de Wal*Mart is like that, and you know that's all you can afford since your latest Dover Saddlery binge.

Why do we feel a need to be so indiscreet about our passion? Who knows? Is this addiction? Who cares? The horse tail big hand on my equestrian-design watch says it's time for *America's Horse* on TV, and I'm betting I'll be Pay-pal-ing another eBay seller before dark. Oh, waiter ... straight jacket, please?

Chapter 20

▼

Talk to the Hoof

(What Farriers Want)

In the July, 2004, issue of *Horse Illustrated* there was an advertisement for a new book. Beats there a horse lover's soul so dead that the promise of a new book won't rouse it? I think not, and I am certainly no exception to "put a horse on it, and they'll buy it" rule. So I pointed and clicked and prepared to order my copy of Millwater Publishing's *10th Anniversary Special Edition New Dictionary of Farrier Terms and Technical Language*. The ad promised "more than 550 terms and definitions with pronunciation guides, additional word origins, new illustrations, updated scientific research and a current directory section". I'm still drooling as I type.

I hustled over to the book's webpage and downloaded a preview. As promised, the preview pages were filled with terms and definitions, pronunciations and cool, in-text black-and-white illustrations so good as to seem three-dimensional. I admit to being a bit taken aback by the definition of *horse*. One would hope that anyone purchasing the book would already have a grip on what to call that big hairy beast out there eating the chrysanthemums. *Horse* is certainly one option.

Not one to quibble, I will say for the book that the section where the parts of a horse's anatomy are detailed may well be worth the $11.95 cover price. There are certain parts of my horses whose precise location has always puzzled me—the kidneys, for instance, and the part of my gelding that makes "that noise" when he trots—and the drawings on the free preview pages were clear and labeled so even I could understand what part was being detailed.

Before I clicked the "Charge It!" button, however, I paused to think about the many conversations, both technical and non, that I've had with my farrier over the years. Most recently we discussed the condition of the front hooves of Zip My Wallet. The gelding isn't a whiner, but he had been suggesting to me that he was not entirely pleased with something going on in his front end. John, his new assistant, Dan, and I hunkered over the offending foot. As Dan scraped away the surface with a hoof knife, a couple of small black lines appeared. "See that?" he said, pointing with the knife.

"What is it?" I asked, waiting for the technical explanation I was sure would follow.

"It's a crack."

"A crack?"

"Like from a stone, you know? A crack." He looked at me over his shoulder as if he was considering sending me for IQ testing. "He must've hit a rock and got a little crack here."

"Oh." Well, I wouldn't call it technical jargon, but a crack by any other name ...

On another day we dealt with the foundered front hooves of my Paint mare, Pokeys Always Pissed. She was foundered when I bought her more than nine years ago, so the care and feeding of her feet has been the number one priority in her care. Each farrier visit brings new and exciting opportunities for pain, real and psychic, and the expenditure of huge sums of cash. On that day too, we three huddled over the hoof as Dan scraped away the outer layer of sole. The red streaks were clearly visible after the first scrape. "Wow! Look at all the bruising!" I said.

"That's where the rotated bone hits the sole," he explained. I watched as he continued to remove sole until the exposed part was pure white. Interested, I waited for further information. None was forthcoming.

"That's really interesting," I prompted.

At that point, John removed Pokey from the crossties with his usual, "Okay, Sparky; you're done," and, as I brought the next victim out of his stall, the conversation drifted to the usual horse-world gossip and silly jokes.

Thinking back, the last time I can recall anything close to technical jargon being used during a farrier session at my barn was when Pokey developed a serious crack in her hoof wall and John told me we might, at some point, have to put screws in it and wire it shut. Not as technical as *hot shoe* or *interdigitate*, but certainly more official than "Okay, Sparky. Let's see that tootsie ..."

I concluded after much deliberation that any technical jargon my farrier needs me to know, he will teach me, just as he has taught me how a horse will stand quietly for him if he rubs his hand on it then lets it sniff the hand. He says this makes him seem like he's somehow related to the horse, since it smells itself on him. Sounds good to me. He has also taught me that the way to gentle a wild horse is to withhold food from it unless you are personally feeding it. That way it connects you with the feeding process and is more likely to let you into its inner circle without kicking your head off. He's taught me that slow and steady doesn't always win the race. Horses seem to distrust anyone who moves *too* slowly, as if they suspect there's a plot afoot to somehow do them damage. Instead, calm, quick, and to the point seems to be the key to keeping horses happy and sane.

My point is not to criticize the publisher of the *Dictionary*. I hope many copies are sold and many farriers are engaged in meaningful, technical conversation by many horse owners. *Salut!* My point is that you never know where the best lessons will be found. John draws pictures in dirt on the rubber mats in my aisleway when he's trying to explain something to me that I'm just not getting. My vet will spend an hour trading horse stories with me in an effort to help me learn why she's doing what she's doing to my horse. Even the farmer who sells me hay has plenty of valuable information to share, and the wonderful man who runs our local farm equipment and feed emporium, is a veritable encyclopedia of useful information and old-time wisdom.

Reading is great; talking the talk is fine, but listening to the wiser, more experienced minds around you is finer yet. I turned to my John and his assistant, Dan, who happened to be under one of my horses at the time. "What," I asked, "would you most like from your clients?"

An important question deserves an important answer, and this one took about an hour the first time around. On his next visit, John delivered to me a bag of goodies. In the bag were three t-shirts bearing slogans appropriate to the shoeing trade and a small stack of books. Three weeks later I am still processing the issue, but feel enlightenment is just around the next bend.

What a horseshoer wants, it seems, is five things:

1. A safe place to work
2. A horse in some reasonable condition and frame of mind for shoeing
3. An owner who understands the basics of how a horse's body parts are connected
4. The courtesy of respect for his time and knowledge
5. Timely payment

What constitutes a safe place to work? Shelter is nice. Most shoers are tough customers, and they can ply their trade pretty much anywhere, but a roof and walls around the work area are a pleasant touch. A fan in the summer heat and a heater in the winter cold are excellent bonuses. Your shoer will probably never complain, but if you want him to stop canceling on sub-zero or 100+-degree days, think about adding those homey touches.

Clear the area. If there are tack trunks (my own personal failure) or odd bits of equipment lying around, a quick move by the horse can entangle both of them or prevent the farrier from being able to escape injury. If your farrier gets injured, you not only have the guilt and legal responsibility of your lapse to deal with, but dozens of irate customers whose horses will be going long and unshod for the duration of his recovery. It's in everyone's best interests for you to keep the area free of crud. Do what the Navy calls a "FOD (foreign object debris) walk-down" before he or she arrives. Anything that doesn't need to be there shouldn't.

While you're remodeling your shoeing area, put in some nice lighting. Being able to see the horse and its feet is key to good farriery. If you don't want overhead lights for whatever reason, run over to Home Depot, Lowe's, or Sears Hardware and pick up a nice work light on a tripod. They're cheap, usually have bright halogen bulbs, and will serve double-duty when you have a late-night vet call to suture up Mr Magic Puffball's latest mystery wound.

The same stores carry nice little refrigerators in which you can store everything from medications to soda and bottled water. At very least, keep some paper cups around or an immersion heater and mugs. Farriery can be thirsty work.

How should you prepare your horse? Well, you can start by going out and getting him from the field before the farrier gets there. Don't leave notes with instructions as to where Loopy Lou can be found. Go find her yourself. Have her reasonably clean and dry and standing in a stall or nearby pen in plenty of time. Many shoers—John is one of them—will not hesitate to go look for your horse, but it's a kindness to everyone involved (including the next horse owner on the day's schedule) if he doesn't have to. Besides, there aren't enough horse shoers as it is. We don't need to be wearing out the ones we've got.

You can probably find a shoer who can handle your unruly horse, but it would be far better if you did some prep work yourself. Granted, all horses will occasionally have a bad day, but the number can be drastically reduced if you regularly pick out your horse's feet so he's used to them being handled. Clicker training is invaluable in this regard. I've spent many happy hours teaching Zip to pick up each hoof and hold it up at a signal. Sometimes he also does it for the farrier. At least he's less likely now to stand stolid and stubborn than he used to be, and the "I dare you!" look has left his eye.

Speaking of clicker training, be careful what you teach. When Baby Doll learned to bow when her front foot was picked up and her body rocked back, it was very cute. When she took it to the next level and also learned to lie down on command, it was even cuter. When the farrier picked up that foot on his next visit and she collapsed on top of him, there wasn't much laughter going on.

Some shoers like the horse loose and held by a lead rope. Others like him cross-tied. A few like a single tie in a stall. You might find one who wants the horse hung upside down from the rafters. Ask your farrier which he prefers, and train your horse to behave in that setting. Again, there will always be bad days. The goal is to limit both their number and their severity.

Don't feed the horse while the shoer is working on him unless you've discussed this in advance. A well-fed horse is more likely to stand quietly, and the temptation to offer hay or grain during shoeing is strong. Unfortunately, the twisting and leaning that result can be hell for the man under the horse.

How do the horse's feet connect to his body? The old adage that "the feet are the horse" is truer than you'd imagine. Among the books in John's goody bag was an old copy of Bud Beaston's *Manual of Problem Horseshoeing* (OK Farrier's College, 1975). If you can find a copy, buy it. Buy it right now. Though methods and materials have evolved since its publication, there is a wealth of knowledge of equine body mechanics to be found within its pages.

I also highly recommend *The Horseshoer*, a text printed for California Polytechnic State University (aka "Cal Poly") in the dark ages, and based on technical manual 2–220 "Prepared under the direction of the Chief of Cavalry, War Department". There is no date on this little book, so you may have to search antique and out-of-print lists to find a copy, but it's worth the effort. The text is short (120 pages), concise and packed with information and line drawings.

In addition, John's bag contained a copy of *The Principles of Horseshoeing*, by Doug Butler, a self-published text dated 1974. This one, too, will be best found in a search of collections of old books, but is no less worth the effort.

I'm sure there are other, more current books on shoeing. They might even be as good. The point is that you need to become familiar not just with the terms shoers use (most avoid using technical language around owners as we tend to misunderstand and get hinky with it), but with the concepts behind the craft.

The way a horse's hoof strikes the ground determines everything from the scope of his movement to the smoothness of his gaits and the alignment of his joints, ligaments, tendons and muscles. Pokey's badly foundered right front foot, for instance, if allowed to grow naturally, causes a dropping of her right heel. That, in turn, puts stress on her flexor tendons, her knee, her right shoulder, her spine, and inevitably turns up as lameness in her right stifle. Considering that, remember that any change in the natural shape or alignment of the hoof will have similar repercussions in your horse's body.

"Some owners at fancy barns decide that if this horse over here has clips, trailers and rolled toes, then their horse should have clips, trailers and rolled toes," John explained. "They don't understand that the clips put pressure on the hoof, and when the shoe finally levers off from the extra leverage of the trailers, they take a chunk of hoof with them. That's fine for a horse that needs that stuff, but not every horse does."

In other words, keeping up with the Joneses' horse is not necessarily a good thing. Just because you saw some fancy shoeing process on a grand prix jumper doesn't mean that copying it will turn your short-strided hacker into Gem Twist. Quite the contrary. The wrong angle of approach to the ground can lame a horse permanently by destroying his knee, shoulder, hock, stifle or back.

Consider the Morgan, "Rat". He was born with a slightly clubbed right forefoot. His feet are hard as rock, and in thirteen years, he has never needed shoes despite the fact that he works hard almost daily. His feet are anything but picture-perfect, which has brought glares of disgust from some quarters at shows, yet he pins well and has never been lame. He paddles, as do many Morgans, so his feet wear on the outside first with flares on the inside. One front foot is slightly more upright than the other.

We could "correct" all of that with trimming and shoeing geared to making him strike the ground evenly all around his hoof. His feet would look pretty, but how long would he last?

Stand up and walk across the room as you normally do. Now, turn your right toes out and try again. Feel the strain on your right knee and hip? Experiment with cotton stuffed under your arch, a heel lift, and something under your toes. Put on high heels (guys, heeled boots will do). Each change in your "shoeing" will create a new way for your foot to strike the ground, and you'll feel it throughout your body. If you've ever had a bad back, arch supports may well be the cure. There's a reason for that, and it applies to your horse as well as to your own body.

There's a movement afoot (no pun intended) for all horses to go barefoot. I confess that, while all of mine are shoeless behind to keep them from injuring each other in the pasture, several of them have front shoes for part of the year, and the foundered mare is never barefoot. Ever. I prefer barefoot horses. Their feet grow naturally, are worn naturally, and their movement is never impaired by human idiocy. Unfortunately, my farm's main crop is rock. The horses that will be ridden on the rocky ground have shoes on in the summer to keep them from bruising. I've tried it both ways, and this is what works in this setting with these horses. Your farrier will guide you when he checks the condition of your horse's feet.

The moral of the story is that it doesn't matter what someone else in the barn is doing or what the current fad on the circuit might be. Your ultimate goal is to keep your horse sound for as long as possible. A horse is a major financial and emotional investment; you don't want to throw it away on a whim. For my money—and for my horses—a good flat-shoer, who trims and shoes with the natural movement of each horse, is worth his weight in apple treats. It's up to each horse owner to be aware of the responsibility to help his horses remain healthy and sound. Beyond that, the choice of shoeing methods is yours.

How can you show respect for your farrier's time and craft? "Don't expect him to help you put hay away after the shoeing," says Dan. More to the point, understand that, though you might find him chatty and fun to have around, his other clients think so, too, and he needs to get to them.

- Don't throw in "just one more horse" when he's finished the twenty you told him about.

- Don't ask him to repair tack or weld the hitch on your trailer.

- Don't harass him with suggestions and critiques.

- Don't tell him what to do unless you're absolutely sure you know more than he does.

- Understand, if he's late, that it's because some other idiot horse owner didn't read this chapter and has him hog-tied twenty miles from your barn.

- If he calls in sick (they rarely do), believe him and just reschedule.

- If you were dumb enough to wait till the day before the show to call him, don't get irritated when he can't squeeze you in. Plan ahead.

- Many farriers take one day off a week. Live with it.

Want to open a charge account? Macy's has some super offers. Your farrier, however, would like to be paid at the time his services are rendered. The time he has to spend chasing down customers who owe him money is time he can't spend under your horses, and every bad debt puts him one step closer to quitting the business and going into something less demanding where he's less likely to have to deal with idiots. He's got expenses to cover. Give him his money and be done with it. You won't earn points by negotiating over prices and payment schedules.

And please stop telling John he doesn't charge enough!

Your farrier doesn't ask much. Allow him his due and deal with his quirks as he deals with yours and those of your rogue ponies. If you don't like the way he shoes, find someone you do like. If you have questions he's not answering, try www.horseshoes.com. A good farrier will answer your questions simply and effectively. A bad one will be immediately apparent. You can fire at will; remember that. Harassment, however, is against the rules. Play fair, and the shoeing process will be a smooth and beneficial one for all involved.

Chapter 21

The Vet's Point-of-View

What does your veterinarian want from you? You get your horses vaccinated, isn't that enough? When Legs Le Roi had that mysterious rash on his nose, you had it checked out, didn't you? What more can you do to make your vet happy and keep him (or her) coming when you call?

Let's talk for a moment about the business end of running a veterinary practice. Be the vet, and look at his day from his perspective.

You've done your stint at college and vet school, and you're proud of what you've accomplished. All you want now is to help animals and make a good living for yourself and your family. You find a location, work out arrangements for a clinic of some sort for in-house procedures, and you outfit a used pickup truck with all the accoutrements that make an on-the-road vet practice viable. You are fully stocked with the basic medications, surgical and first aid equipment, vaccines, and the necessary random bits for their application. From balling guns to Vetwrap, you're armed for battle.

You might have bought a practice from a retiring vet, or you might join a multi-vet practice. If you have some financial backing, you might start out all on your own, but that's the exception rather than the rule. You've got a cell phone, and it's already ringing as your name is being handed out by other vets you've met who have clients they need to get rid of (either due to numbers or attitudes). What might you not want to hear when you answer that phone?

How about this: "Hi. I need you here *now!* It's an *emergency!* Soup Bone just came in from the pasture with Lyme Disease! Fever? Uh … I don't know. I'm feeling her forehead, but I can't tell if it's hot. Pulse? She's standing, so she must have one! How does she look? Like a horse! What do you mean what makes me think she's got Lyme Disease? She's got a tick on her, and she's kind of—you know—funny."

At this point you are feeling a bit depressed. You check the schedule, find that you have an appointment to geld a yearling in two hours. The client on the phone is twenty minutes away. You press for more information so you can do a little long-distance triage. Is this horse sick enough to warrant calling the colt's owners and begging for time? What to do?

You'd be able to answer that question in a blink if the guy on the phone had bothered to gather his information *before* he called. The horse isn't bleeding or down and thrashing, so he had the time to take her temperature and her pulse and record the readings. He could be a new horse owner, but for heaven's sake! When he's sick he takes his own temperature and knows about where his pulse might be. Why didn't he do the same for the mare? Could he have at least been alert enough to notice things like whether or not the horse was sweating or wobbling or losing body parts? Could he have taken a moment to walk the horse around and determine if there really was anything wrong other than a tick snacking on her chest?

You make the decision to postpone the gelding until you can assess the mare, and off you go, already knowing it's going to be a long afternoon.

The cell phone continues to ring. What else would you not want to hear? How about, "Soooooooo, you're the new vet, eh? Are you enjoying working around here? Where did you move from? Oh! Sure! The horse has been lying down chewing on his belly for about two days. I don't think it's anything important; after all, I give them all a bran mash twice a week. Saw that in *Horse Alive* last year and been doin' it ever since. Colic? Nah.

My horses never colic. Why don't you c'mon over and take a look when you have a minute. I just want to be sure he hasn't got EPQSLM2, or whatever that new disease is called. Read about it in last month's *Equine Stuff*."

Well, this one sounds like a definite emergency even though the owner doesn't think so. You call both of the other clients, tell them you'll be late, and turn the truck around. This horse is an hour in the other direction.

At the end of the day, after having assessed and treated the horses and calmed the owners, what are you likely to hear? "Why are you charging me for an emergency call? My horse wasn't sick till you got here! He's never colicked in his life!" and "Really? You have to do a blood test for Lyme? I don't know … how much does that cost?" Only the colt's owner, who is in a coma from having sat in the hot sun waiting for you, is pleased as punch with whatever you did. For this you gave up dancing for Chippendale's!

Roll back the tape, and look at a good vet day.

The phone rings, and you hear, "Hi! Spooky is down and breathing hard. His respiration rate is 34, his temp is 102, and his capillary refill rate is poor. He's got a bounding pulse in his left fore. When I can get him to stand, he's disoriented and weak-kneed. I'll be here with him. When can you get here?"

Now *that's* an emergency call any vet can love! Not that emergency calls are pleasant, but they're going to happen, and having all the information up front makes the job of assessing the severity of the problem a lot easier. With that kind of report, the question of which horse to postpone and which to deal with immediately is fairly clear-cut. There may still be issues—two emergencies at once when both are life-threatening can make you grey before dinner—but at least you have all the necessary information to begin the process. You can give the owner instructions by phone to keep the animal alive until you get there. You haven't wasted time in irritating chit-chat, nor have you been left trying to second-guess the owner.

Which client are you? Do you know the basics of equine first aid? If not, what are you doing owning a horse? The fact that you were able to keep a goldfish alive for two years means nothing to your horse or his doctor.

You need to remember the following: Horses can't talk. In order for the vet to do his job, he has to read the horse's body. He may not know your horse, but you do. If Purse Strings has always had a crooked left front leg, you know that. If Fuzzbutt always reacts with hives after lime is spread on the pasture, you should know that too. You need to know your horse and know basic care techniques so that you and your vet can work as a team to keep the animal healthy and above-ground.

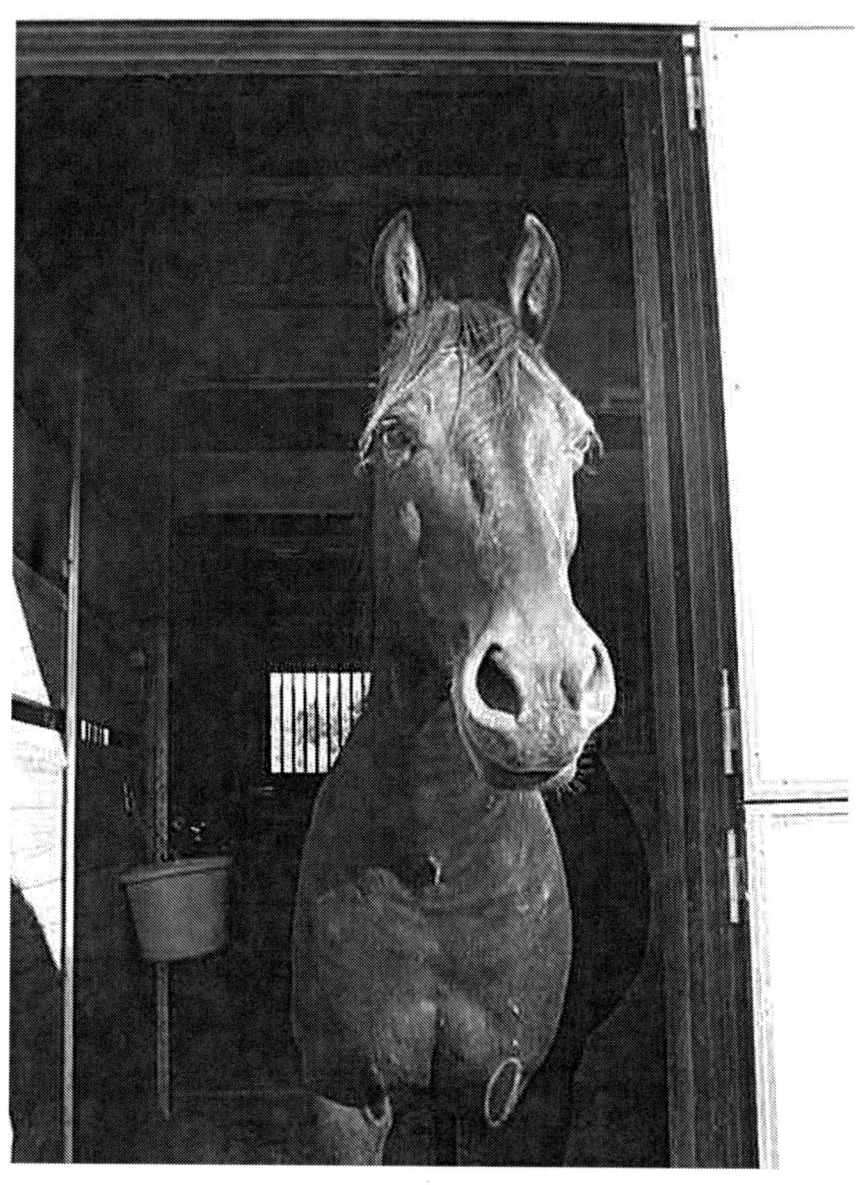

*Sadly, Willowrock Ultimately suffered from Macronomia.
As "The Rat" he really blossomed.*

CHAPTER 22

▼

STRANGE EQUINE AFFLICTIONS

First-time horse owners are frequently baffled and shocked by the odd maladies that afflict their new horses. My own panic when I arrived at the boarding farm to find my first horse apparently dead in her stall has not been forgotten. Nor has the barn manager's hysterical laughter as she assessed the corpse. "She's sleeping. You've ridden the piss out of her, and she's having a nap."

There are lots of veterinary guides and manuals available, and I highly recommend that all horse owners buy several. They are fascinating and full of good information about serious ailments, and they lend a bit of class to dinner-party conversation. I suggest that you buy a leather-bound one with color photographs as well as line drawings. It will be far more expensive, which is in keeping with the "Nothing is Too Good for My Horse" policy stamped across your new breed-specific credit card.

While you're waiting for the books to arrive, I want to share some information on several of the more intriguing ailments your horse will likely present within fifteen minutes of delivery.

Allergies: Horses get hay fever. They sneeze, cough, and blow mucous on your new riding shirt. Not all of them will get this, but yours probably will. It costs a lot to control allergies, so they are favored by many very inexpensive horses as a way to make their owners feel special.

Bony Head Syndrome: The primary symptom is a black eye and swollen cheek. You will develop these when your horse's head occupies the same space as your face. This happens most often during grooming and tacking-up. Treatment is the same as when you tried your son's skateboard in the driveway. The horse's head is supposed to be that hard.

Carrotismus: The symptoms are few and distinctive, including orange-colored saliva and a refusal to work without a bribe. Treatment includes cold-turkey withdrawal from hand-fed treats. Occasionally horses will cure themselves by stealing an intact carrot from your pocket and choking to death.

Castration Complex: Suffered mostly by the male partners of female horse owners. The horse generally recovers quickly from castration ("gelding" as we in the trade call it). Men generally don't. He may exhibit skittishness and phantom pain, particularly if he was a witness to the event. Similar but less severe symptoms may be evidenced after he has watched you clean your gelding's sheath.

Dysphonia: When you call your horse in the pasture, and he ignores you until you walk the four thousand feet to where he's grazing, then appears startled that you are in the neighborhood, he is not deaf. In humans, this is called "selective listening". In horses it is normal, though often thought to be related to gelding.

Dystonia: The same horse who just spent twenty minutes galloping wildly around the pasture while you followed with halter and lead dragging behind you will, in the arena, be incapable of anything faster than a walk. He may, in fact, fall asleep at the halt. Acute cases pass quickly upon application of "leg aids". Chronic cases are expensive to treat as they require that you buy a new horse.

Equine Ericalosis: The only person who can ride your retired grand-prix horse without being lawn-darted into the emergency room is the barn owner's four-year-old daughter, Erica. Symptoms include bucking, rearing, cursing, crying, and paying huge amounts of money for more training. The affliction will not be resolved until you give your horse to Erica and buy a new one.

Fragrant Desuscitation: This is a completely benign condition. Your horse is not ill. His breath is supposed to smell like that. He will share it with you at every opportunity, so get used to it. If you wish to treat the horse anyway, mints will suffice.

Frequent Flatulation: There are actual equine illnesses that will cause endless and well-timed farting. Sharing your lunch with your horse, accidentally or on purpose, can also cause gastric distress which will result in creation of mega-gas. Too much spring grass will result in flatulence accompanied by projectile diarrhea (which, by the way, will be green—a nice touch as it blends well with Tailored Sportsman breech colors). It is my considered opinion that "jet propelled" horses are able to control their expulsiveness, and use that fact to their advantage in confined spaces. Nothing says "School's out!" like an owner passed out on the floor of the barn aisle in mid-tack-up.

Graduated Gynasthesia: Your mare really was easy to handle when she lived with her last owner. She did not develop an overwhelming need to get laid until you bought her. Rumor has it that breeding her will help her get over her "mare-ish-ness" and return her to her prior, semi-somnolent state. I haven't noticed an improvement myself. I suspect the treatment plan was devised by a committee of men.

Gradyosis: Named after my daughter's aged gelding, this bizarre affliction is the result of **Nocturnal Mysterymia** in a horse suffering from **Bony Head Syndrome**. The affected horse will return from a night in the pasture with a lump the size of Wisconsin on his face and no other symptoms. Panic will ensue in all human quarters. Diagnosis requires that multiple specimens be taken for testing, vets and scientists the world over consulted, and lengthy discussions launched with anyone who has even seen a horse and is willing to look at the awesome digital pictures you've taken with your new camera. This is not a malignant growth. It is, in fact, just as it appears: a lump. Treatment involves several martinis and the installation of a night-vision camera in the pasture to prevent further problems. NOTE: An unusual side-effect might be noticed as afflicted horses frequently develop an irrational fear of veterinary jumpsuits.

Hackophasia: The horse appears lame or launches into bucking and rearing fits only (and always) when you ride out on the trail. He's forgotten how much fun it can be to haul you and your equipment over miles of rocky terrain, in and out of rivers and streams, and through bug-infested forests in all kinds of weather. This is not a physical ailment. You can buy back his affection by leading him onto the trail and feeding him apple chunks every hundred feet. Or you can buy a new horse.

Girth Itch: This is a real ailment. If the horse is irritated by the girth, check to see whether or not it is rubbing a sore spot or causing a rash. Treatment is imperative. The condition is easily transmitted from equine to human in the form of **Hematoma Grande**. Even in the cross-ties, an irritable horse can reach around and nip or kick the crud out of you if he is not happy. A new, chafeless girth is cheaper than the co-pay at the ER.

Ickynastymalaura: Horses are prone to the proliferation of stuff that is nasty to look at, bad-smelling, and defies identification. Most of these things are normal. Occasionally one of them is not. That's why you paid the big bucks for the leather-bound vet manual with the color photos. If you're uncertain whether the stuff coming from or growing on your horse is deadly, stop reading this book and go get that one.

Justin Morgan Syndrome: Justin Morgan had a horse. That doesn't mean that you must have one too. In its human form, this illness causes irrational purchase of multiple equines. The equine version causes horses to become overly curious, too enthusiastic, and too smart for their saddles. Treatment options are limited. Buying another horse will only cause the illness to progress more quickly.

Kelso's Disease: Primarily afflicts older horses who should have more sense than to race the new two-year-old to the gate. Symptoms include abrasions and contusions, rapid pulse and respiration, and occasionally a broken fence post.

Lameness: This is a vast category of ailments, some real and some imagined. Briefly, if the horse appears to be walking funny, it probably is. If it wasn't lame until you brought out the saddle, at which time your horse did a passable version of the death scene from *Camille*, he's probably faking it. It is often possible to determine the level of lameness by turning the horse out into the pasture and screaming "Dinner!" We've also had good luck staring the horse in the eye and whispering "Alpo!" Lameness is often not in the limb in which it appears to be, which can lead to much hilarity. Causes can range from a bruised foot through soft-tissue damage to broken bones, though all are avoidable if you get out of the way *before* you yell "Dinner!" Lameness is best treated by a trained professional. Forget the book and actually call the vet.

Macronomia: Unique to very small or ugly horses with overly-long, too-elegant names. Symptoms include depression and refusal to acknowledge verbal commands (see **Dysphonia**).

Neoplasma: Unrelated to "neoplastic", which is a big, important word indicating a tumorous condition requiring veterinary care, **Neoplasma** has as its primary symptom a lethargy brought on by the discovery that the barn next door has a new plasma-screen TV for the horses' viewing pleasure while yours has only windows and a radio. Horses are easily spoiled, so it is not recommended that you treat this ailment by applying credit cards. Instead, increase stimulating bonding time by sitting in the barn reading aloud from *The Black Stallion*.

Otolaryngeal Murkiness: There is a connection between the horse's ear and its nasal passages that will cause the production and discharge of copious stringy mucous upon mention of show season or phone conversations with potential buyers. Treatment options include fuzzy balls stuffed in the horse's ears. This should suffice until he learns to lip-read, at which point the condition becomes chronic and incurable.

Partradean Miasma: Similar in symptoms to **Neoplasma**, this condition results from the discovery by your equine that the expensive horse in the next stall has much better stuff than your horse's owner is willing to spring for. Depression and an unwillingness to leave the barn in daylight are typical indications of this syndrome.

Tail-swishing: This is a symptom, not a disease, though it is often mislabeled due to the accompanying cough which recent research suggests is actually the sound of your horse laughing. If your cheeks are turning streaky red due your horse's uncanny ability to time his "flay swatting" to coincide with your hindquarters-grooming efforts, your horse has mastered tail swishing. Accepted treatments include clicker training and tying his tail to his legs with baling twine. Duct tape is not recommended as it can turn a fly-away tail into a bat, which will cause far greater damage.

Variable Appendagitis: This condition is often mistaken for lameness, which it closely resembles. The main symptom is the feeling that the horse has grown an extra leg in the middle of a complicated dressage move or on the approach to a new jump. Either one or a brief flurry of oddly-rhythmed strides will cause you to pull up and dismount to count legs. If there are six—two of yours and four of his—he is suffering from this uncommon and intriguing disease.

Zygotaesthemia: You bred your highly-paperd bay mare to your neighbor's incentive fund bay stud, and the resulting foal is a dapple grey with ears like a donkey. Also known as "misplaced zygote syndrome", this often results from the mare having made a midnight call on the ugly horse tied to the tree in front of the ramshackle travel trailer three lots down. There's no accounting for taste, but this hardly qualifies as an ailment.

There are many, many more ailments and conditions about which you will learn courtesy of your new horse. Remember, there are no perfect horses, only perfect fools who believe there are.

Only maturity can carry off a dapper look like this.

Chapter 23

This Old Horse

(and Other Myths)

The daily mail inevitably brings one or another ad for a "nutraceutical" guaranteeing a cure for what ails my horses. I'm on a mailing list somewhere, and it's been distributed far and wide. It's no surprise, since by morning I will probably have ordered one of everything in the flyer. I may not, at the moment, have horses suffering from the illnesses and troubles described by any given manufacturer, but I might. My horses are a lot like me: a little long in the tooth, loose in the butt, and headed for the shady side of the pasture. We're all aging together, and for my money, there can't be enough medical miracles to see us all through to a peaceful ending. I'm not about to let one pass us by.

I noticed there's been a change in the kinds of ads I get, and I'm going to hazard a guess that they reflect not so much a change in the approach of medical science (and pseudo-science, in some cases), but an acceptance by the Marketing Gods that the graying of America brings with it an avid desire among us baby boomers to avoid death and the icky stuff that leads to it.

We're getting older, but we're staying fit longer. That means we're riding longer, and the horses we own are being treated to the benefits of our goal-driven behavior. The same medical miracles that are keeping the world's citizens hale and hearty into their 80's and 90's are keeping horses alive well into their 30's. Back in the day, a rider—especially a female rider—past 60 was considered a marvel, and a horse nearing 20 was pretty much retired. Last year, when my idol, cowgirl and riding instructor Connie Reeves, of San Antonio, Texas, died at the age of 101 in a fall from her 30-plus-year-old trail horse, the news came in a short article in a horse magazine and an even shorter on in the *New York Times*, whose front page, I believe, it might have landed on a generation ago. I was saddened, but not for long. She'd had an admirably long run, and I was full of enthusiasm at the thought that one day I, too, might be sitting a horse at an age when my mother's generation wouldn't even have been around to drool into their oatmeal.

Which brings me back to mail-order health. Years ago, the ads I received were fewer, and they tended towards the "See your horse's coat shine like the sun!" type of product push. Today's ads are more along the line of "Arthritis doesn't need to mean the end for your equine pal". And the manufacturers have wised up enough to be creating identical products for equines, their humans, and any and all other pets we've got limping around us. We're all drifting into our dotage together, and it's lovely that we can all pop the same pills for the same problems. What a bonding experience!

While we're on the subject of aging, I firmly believe that horse psychology is never as important as when we are dealing with aging equines. Anyone who has owned a horse for a number of years has had the startling experience of the instant aging process. With our relatively long life spans, we humans come gradually from the light into the shadows. A little arthritis here, a cataract there, perhaps a bit of hearing loss take us slowly from full function to partial disability over a period of a decade or more. Our horses are not that lucky.

The shorter life span of horses—of most animals, for that matter, apart from my deafeningly loud and obnoxious parrot-type bird (as described in the *Big Book of Birds*) who will outlive me or kill me trying—makes the aging process appear rather brief and sudden. One day Sonny Boy is ripping blankets and fly masks off his herd mates with abandon; the next he's spending hours in the shade of his favorite tree and grumbling at the horse shoer. It's a sad fact but true: Horses get old.

My personal herd is on the long-in-the-tooth end of the equine life continuum. The youngest is nine and beginning to lose his adolescent silliness. The oldest is coming twenty-seven and sporting fused hock joints, opaque lenses, a heart murmur, and the open-mouthed, pellet-spewing gumming that passes for chewing in horses with only a few teeth left. Between the two are the heave-y mare, the Quarter Horse with the stiff rear, the Thoroughbred with the clicking stifle, the Appy whose one good eye is beginning to cloud.

For those of us who have the luxury (and incredibly hard work) of keeping our horses at home, the choice is simple. We make sure the vet is aware of impending problems, change feed rations, give the old guys their choice of paddocks or pastures in which to loll away the hours, and prepare for the end as best we can.

Horse owners who board their horses out, however, are at a disadvantage when the twilight begins to fall in their best friends' eyes. The question of whether to keep the horse and give up a preferred riding discipline (or riding at all, in some cases) or to send him on to cheaper pastures is one that preys on owners' minds.

The options for someone in this situation are limited. The horse can be retired at a reduced monthly rate to a farm where his biggest challenge will be finding a place to sleep during the day. Assuming he is "serviceably sound", he can be donated to a program for handicapped riders. He can be given away as a companion horse or "for limited riding only". He can be euthanized.

There are variations on the theme, but in general, those are the choices. The last, of course, is the one we all avoid for as long as possible. To euthanize a reasonably sound horse just goes against the grain. Horse people are soft touches with their hearts where their brains should be. If they weren't, no one would own an animal that spends 80% of his time eating and making piles of manure and 90% of his owner's income doing so. We'll leave that option on the list, but I'm not going to discuss it at great length.

That still leaves choices. Which to choose …? Which to choose …?

Obviously money is a huge factor in this decision. Retirement facilities are often wonderful places for our equine friends. The care can be excellent (check out the place before you send Fluffy there, however, or you may be unpleasantly surprised), and your horse can enjoy his final years in a setting that is as stress-free and healthful as circumstances allow.

Excellent care, however, can be a two-edged sword. Sure, you want your baby taken care of, but be sure you have a plan in mind for the time when constant veterinary supervision might be required. Then there's the longevity issue. My boarder, Pinky the One-Eyed Wonder App, is twenty-five now. He was only fifteen when he came here to retire. He's a solid, healthy animal who may well go on for more years than his owner would care to think about. She's been paying board without complaint for ten years. Granted, it's cheap board, but it's a monthly expense that looks as if it will go on forever. Make sure you're prepared to pay for however many years that excellent care might buy your horse. She's into this retirement process for nearly $20,000 in board alone. Add vet calls, annual shots, blankets, farrier and dentist bills, and the sum begins to look unpleasantly like the window sticker on a new car. I'm not suggesting that you cheap out; just that you look at the bottom line realistically.

Donating a horse to charity is another option with an up and a down side. I've experienced the down side, and I'm here to tell you it's the stuff nightmares are made of. The handsome Appy gelding I donated to a respected handicapped program had been diagnosed with navicular syndrome. I had three horses boarded and couldn't afford to keep one who was in danger of becoming permanently lame. Besides, I figured that light work with light riders could prolong his life and make it worth living. The deal was struck, and off he went to his new digs, not thrilled, but willing to give it a shot. I rested easy knowing he'd be well-managed in a place with a vet and farrier on staff and certified trainers.

It was only last year that I found out that the place had closed just two years after that donation. I will never know what happened to my boy in the intervening decade, and I will have occasional teary moments. That doesn't make all donations questionable; I present it to give pause to an owner who might go blindly down that aisle.

The up side of donation is that there are many, many good quality facilities and programs in need of solid lesson horses. The service they provide is invaluable to the handicapped riders who adore them. There can be many good years ahead for a slightly damaged animal with a good attitude, and it may well be worth the risk to give him that chance.

Giving away a horse as a "companion" can also have good and bad results. I nearly took in a wonderful Thoroughbred gelding a few years ago. His owner wanted nothing more than a good home for him, and I certainly had enough room and energy to deal with an aging equine. The problem came in the form of stipulations. The owner, delighted with my enthusiastic response, hugged me, then read me the litany of activities I could *not* do with the horse. The animal was sound with a "little suspensory issue", but the owner did not want him doing dressage, jumping, trail riding or giving lessons. That left walk/trot in the ring.

Now, you're probably thinking, "So, you took the horse and did what you wanted with him, right? What would the owner know?" Wrong. The owner lived around the corner and was planning weekly visits to check on her boy. I opted out of that situation without hesitation. An overly anxious mommy watching our every move would not a pleasant partnership make.

If you give a horse away, he belongs to the new owner. You may have a contract drawn up that gives you the right to take him back under certain circumstances, or you might ask for right of first refusal if he's eventually put on the market, but you can't expect the new owner to deal with daily visits and a report card at the end of the month. Make sure you know what your feelings are about the horse's new situation before you strike a deal. Afterwards is too late.

I've seen horses half-leased to young riders to help defray board costs, and I've seen them sent to live with relatives. Mares, if they're lame but not too old can go for breeding, though that's not always a cushy existence.

Geldings tend to be a drug on the market once they are no longer serviceable in the riding scheme of things.

This is not a sales pitch for backyard horsekeeping, by any means. I'm lucky, and I know it. All that advertising for supplements and treatments has not fallen on deaf ears here, and I'm able to maintain the ridiculous feeding and treating schedule that a cluster of whiny pensioners require. As a result, my horses and I are at peace, and they will probably live long enough to become an intolerable burden on my own aging body. That's okay. I figure it's what I deserve for playing with horses for so long.

Most important, though, is the fact that my horses, in their dotage, will not be subjected to sudden environmental changes. There won't be any working their way into a new herd or learning their way around a new pasture. If there's an area in which we most need to be sensitive to old horses, it's not in their aches and pains so much as it's in their peace of mind. A young horse may have a hard time adjusting to a new home, but he'll get over it. An old horse may or may not. I figure any horse that's belonged to one person for more than ten years is going to be a hard sell when it comes to moving on. Maybe I'm wrong. I've been known (though I won't admit it) to anthropomorphize from time to time. Maybe I'm only imagining that horses are creatures of habit who despise chaos and disruption ... nah! I know in my heart I'm right. It's nearly five o'clock, and half of my herd is lined up at the gate for supper. The old guy who heads the group will enter his stall first, followed by his girlfriend, the ever-lovely Baby Doll. The others will sort themselves into their assigned places in their assigned order, leaving only Zips A Turkey to play jokes on them by visiting each of their stalls and taking a mouthful of their feed. Even *that* is habit! Who wants to mess with perfection?

Old horses are even-tempered (though that temper may be chronically bad) and have nothing left to prove. They are happy to oblige. They make great pets. The decisions we make on their behalf need to be as balanced and reasonable as the horses themselves. Remember: that flashy youngster is not going to be happy sitting in the sun with you while you try to remember where you left your saddle. For that, you need an old horse....

and as many supplements as you can find to keep you both trotting into the sunset for years to come.

Chapter 24

Messy Endings

It's impossible to write about the insanity of horse love without coming up against that horrific, terrible, heart-rending subject of the departure of a beloved (or even a not-so-beloved) equine. Someone once said that death is part of life, and that's a great a truth as any I've heard including "manure happens".

If you're very, very lucky, your horse will pass away in the night, leaving you bereft but secure in the knowledge that you did not have a direct hand in his demise. It is my dream to—just once—call the horses for breakfast and have the oldest, most infirm of the bunch just not show up. I'd like to be one of those lucky souls who walk into the pasture in search of the missing equine and find him at peace under his favorite tree, a smile on his lips and a last mouthful of grass still stuck between his teeth. I know that, for me, at least, this will never happen. My horses have never been into happy endings.

I haven't lost all that many horses, so I'm not in any way an expert in horse passing, but I have lost enough. One is too many. Two or three leave you glowering up there at the top of the "wish I didn't ever have to do this again" list.

The first horse I lost was my favorite mare. I'd no sooner bought the farm and contracted for the big, fancy barn to be built than I got the call at work. "You'd better get over here." Colic doesn't begin to describe it. Every blade of grass that entered her mouth sent her into a cold, writhing sweat. I watched helplessly as she rolled on the ground, staring at me with blank, pain-deadened eyes. For two weeks the vets worked at finding out what was causing this sudden (we'd been running barrels only two weeks earlier) and unaccustomed (she'd only had one emergency vet call in the nine years I'd owned her) devastation. In the end, a midnight run to the vet hospital and a thousand more dollars of testing proved only that she would starve to death in agony if left to her own devices. I gave the word, and she was gone. The autopsy showed cancer lesions in her gut. I was relieved of the title Bad Horse Mommy, but not of the pain of having made that call.

The second time around it was cancer again. Six months of insanity—x-rays, biopsies, treatments—and we still didn't know what was happening. The vet had *me* on speed dial! Rushing home after work to treat or feed the old-timer became so much a part of my life that the day after he was finally put to rest, I had to force myself to go shopping so that I wouldn't rush home and face that empty stall. It took two full weeks to adjust my schedule. It will take far longer for the hole in my life to close up.

In the years between the two I watched my friends deal with their sick and dying equines. Not one of them went quietly in the night. They all put up a fuss. They all turned their owners' lives to chaos before they left. They all asked for the human they depended on to make that final call.

I'm telling you this because it's one point that is often missed in the rush to buy a horse. When we're standing in the aisle of the sale barn fondling the thick forelock of the pony that is already making our child grin before we've even signed the check, the farthest thing from our besotted thoughts is what we'll do when it's time to say goodbye. Yet, that's always the end of the story. We need to remember that.

There are lots of alternatives for avoiding the inevitable. We can send our pensioners off to a retirement farm where they will live out their days and be quietly put down without our having to actually look them in the eye at that final moment. We can trade up when our horses pass a certain age so that, with luck, we'll never have one that will reach that sundown moment. We can make all the accommodations we can think of to get around it, but nothing guarantees that we'll be immune.

Not long ago a foal was cruelly shot in the pasture as he stood peacefully with his dam. The dam was killed; the yearling seriously injured. Another yearling tried to follow his owner out the escape door of a four-horse, straight-load trailer at a show He didn't quite clear the chest bar, got hung up by the tie attached to his halter, and severed his leg in his attempts to get free. He was—after several hours of standing around while the owner's partner was contacted for insurance purposes—euthanized right there next to the warm-up ring. He'd won his class. His owner was disconsolate, moaning and screaming on her knees on the ground.

They get us, these horses of ours, no matter how fast we run or how low we duck. They see us coming, and they aim all that trust and affection right at us, and they get us in the heart. We need to remember and be prepared. If you can't stand the heat, get out of the barn. If you can, just keep in mind that they look to us for care and trust us not to hurt them, but part of that is keeping them from dying in pain and without dignity.

To paraphrase the poet, Rudyard Kipling:

> When the body that lived at your single will,
> With its nicker of welcome, is stilled (how still!)
> When the spirit that answered your every mood
> Is gone—wherever it goes—for good,
> *You will discover how much you care,*
> *And will give your heart to a HORSE to tear.*

["The Power of the Dog", Rudyard Kipling]

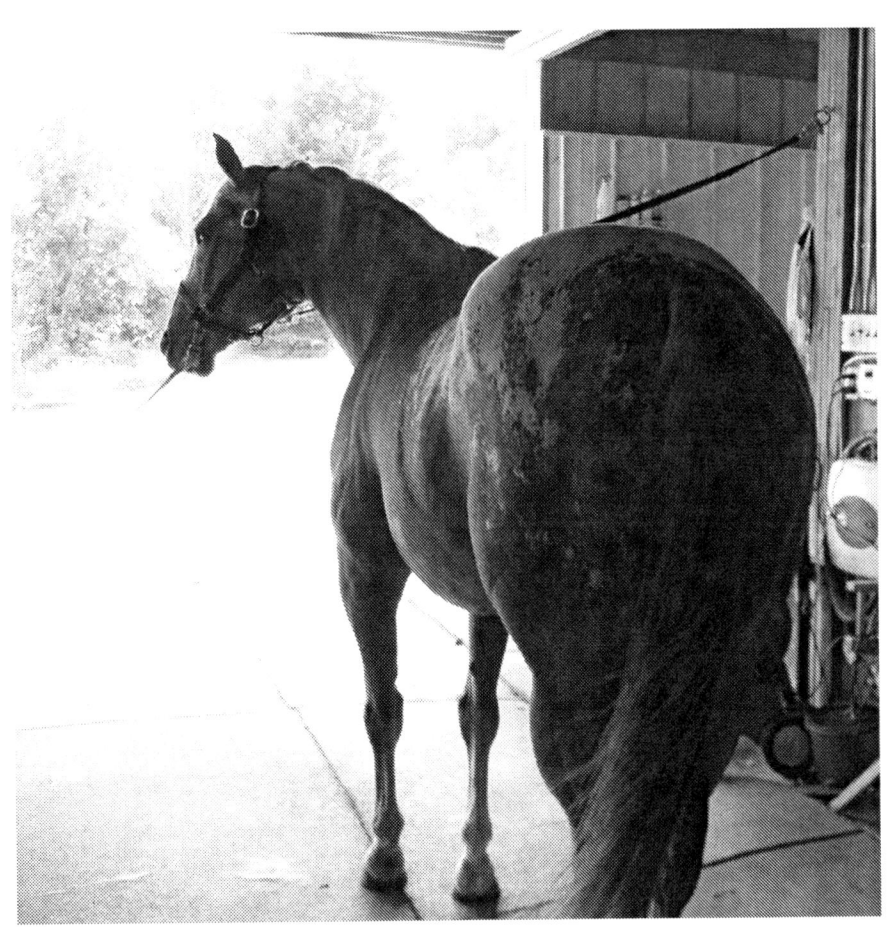

Connected to Nature but content to be out of the heat

Chapter 25

Epilogue

If any of the advice and cautionary tales in this book have touched, taught, or tickled you, then I've done what I set out to do. If you've decided to throw caution to the wind and take a horse into your life, you are in excellent company and will be rewarded a thousand fold for your generosity of spirit (not to mention donation of your paycheck now and your sanity forever into the future).

Horses present humans with dilemmas galore, but taken in the spirit in which they are created, every instance of chaos holds at its core a lesson we need to learn. I've often wondered what people without animals do for comic relief and how they learn where they really fit in this world. Like all wild creatures, horses are deeply connected to the earth and equine spirit animates its small corner of that entirety with great flare and beauty. Taken as a whole the human/horse experience is chaotic and beautiful and worthy. Enjoy the moments; they are rare gems worth treasuring.

978-0-595-46285-8
0-595-46285-5

LaVergne, TN USA
27 August 2009

155988LV00008B/2/A